# 1000 THINGS YOU SHOULD KNOW ABOUT

# GEOGRAPHY

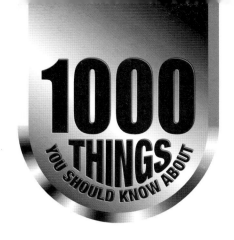

# GEOGRAPHY

## John Farndon

PUBLISHING

First published by
Miles Kelly Publishing Ltd
Bardfield Centre, Great Bardfield, Essex, CM7 4SL

Copyright © Miles Kelly Publishing 2000

2 4 6 8 10 9 7 5 3 1

**Project Manager:** Ian Paulyn
**Art Director:** Clare Sleven
**Editorial Director:** Paula Borton
**Production:** Rachel Jones
**Artwork Commissioning:** Susanne Grant, Lynne French
**Assistants:** Lesley Cartlidge, Liberty Mella
**Additional Design:** Thomas Keenes
Written and designed by John Farndon and Angela Koo
for Barnsbury Books

British Library Cataloguing-in-Publication Data
A catalogue record for this book is available from the British library

ISBN 1-902947-73-8

Printed in Hong Kong

# CONTENTS

J127,889
£10·20

**KEY**

 Asia

 The Americas

 Europe

 Africa and Australasia

 People

 Places

# The Alps

▲ *The pointed summit of the Matterhorn is the third highest peak of the Alps.*

- **The Alps** are Europe's largest mountain range, 1,000 km long, up to 250 km wide and covering 210,000 sq km.

- **The highest Alpine peak** is Mont Blanc (4,807 m) on the France-Italy-Switzerland border.

- **Famous peaks** include the Matterhorn (4,478 m) and Monte Rosa (4,807 m) on the Swiss-Italian border.

- **The Alps began to form** about 70 million years ago when the African crustal plate shifted into Europe.

- **The Alps are the source** of many of Europe's major rivers such as the Rhine, Rhone, Po and Danube.

- **Warm, dry, violent winds** called föhns blow down northern slopes, melting snow and starting avalanches.

- **The high Alpine pastures** are famous for their summer grazing for dairy cows. In winter, the cows come down into the valleys. This is called transhumance.

- **The Alps** are being worn away by human activity. In valleys, cities and factories are growing, while skiing wears away the slopes at the tops of the mountains.

- **The Alps** have the world's highest vineyards, 1,500 m up.

# Thailand and Burma

▶ *Many canals thread through Bangkok and provide a way for poor people to bring goods to sell.*

- **Thailand:** Capital: Bangkok. Population: 59.7 million. Currency: Baht. Language: Thai.

- **Burma:** Capital: Rangoon. Population: 44.6 million. Currency: Kyat. Language: Burmese.

- **In 1990** the National League for Democracy (NDL) led by Aung San Suu Kyi won free elections in Burma but the army has kept them out of power ever since.

- **Burma's military** leaders call the country Myanmar.

- **Growing opium poppies** to make the painkiller morphine and the drug heroin is one of the few ways the people of north Burma can make money.

- **The world's best rubies** come from Mogok in Burma.

- **Thailand's capital** is called Bangkok by foreigners but its real name has over 17 words beginning 'Krungthep', so many locals call it Krung Thep.

- **Most people in Thailand** and Burma still live in the countryside growing rice to eat.

- **Most people** live on fertile plains and deltas – around the Irrawaddy River in Burma and the Chao Phraya in Thailand.

- **Millions** of tourists come to Thailand each year to visit the country's beaches, and the attractions of the city of Bangkok.

# Greece

- **Capital:** Athens. Area: 131,957 sq km. Currency: Drachma. Language: Greek.

- **Physical features:** Highest mountain: Mt Olympus (2,917 m).

- **Population:** 10.6 million. Population density: 79/sq km. Life expectancy: men 75.6 years; women 80.7 years.

- **Wealth:** GDP: $122.4 billion. GDP per head: $11,640.

- **Exports:** Clothes, olive oil, marble, petroleum products, fruit and tobacco.

- **Farming:** Greece is so mountainous that only a third can be

▼ Greece is one of the most mountainous countries in Europe.

farmed, but a third of all workers work on the land, many raising goats or growing olives or vines for wine.

- **Greece** is the world's third largest grower of olives after Spain and Italy.

- **Greek salad** includes olives and feta cheese from goats milk. In some small villages, bakers allow villagers to cook their food in their *fuorno* oven.

- **More than 10 million** visitors come to Greece each year – some to see the relics of Ancient Greece, but most to soak up the sun.

- **Athens** is the ancient capital of Greece, dominated by the Acropolis with its famous Parthenon temple ruins. Athens is also a modern city, with pollution caused by heavy traffic.

# World trade

- **International trade** is the buying and selling of goods and services between different countries.

- **International trade** has increased so much people talk of the 'globalization' of the world economy. This means that goods are sold around the world.

- **The balance of world trade** is tipped in favour of the world's richest countries and companies.

- **Just 200 huge multinational** companies control much of world trade.

- **Just five countries** – the USA, Germany, Japan, France and the UK – control almost half world trade.

- **The 23 richest countries** control 74% of world trade.

- **The 40 poorest countries** control just 5% of world trade.

- **Some countries** rely mainly on just one export. 98% of Nigeria's export earnings come from oil; 80% of Ghana's come from cocoa.

- **Some countries** such as the USA want 'free trade' – that is, no restrictions on trade; other less powerful nations want tariffs (taxes on foreign goods) and quotas (agreed quantities) to protect their home industries.

- **The World Trade Organization** was founded on Jan 1, 1995 to police world trade, and to push for free trade.

▼ This diagram shows the proportions of each kind of good traded around the world.

Mining 9.3%

Other 2.1%

Manufacturing 57.3%

Farming 9.4%

Services 21.9%

# Peoples of northern Asia

- **83% of Russians** are descended from a group of people called Slavs who first lived in eastern Europe 5,000 years ago.

- **East Slavs** are the Great Russians (or Russians), the Ukrainians and the Belorussians (or White Russians).

- **West Slavs** are eastern Europeans such as Czechs, Poles and Slovaks.

▲ *The Kazakhs or Cossacks were famous for their horseriding skills.*

- **South Slavs** are Balkan people such as Croats, Serbs and Slovenes.

- **Slavs speak** Slavic or Slavonic languages such as Russian, Polish or Czech.

- **In the old Soviet Union** there were over 100 ethnic groups. 70% were Slavs. Many of the rest were Turkic people such as Uzbeks, Kazakhs and Turkmen. Many of these peoples now have their own nations.

- **Slavic** people are mainly Christian; Turkic people are mainly Islamic.

- **Many Turkic peoples** such as the Kazakhs have a nomadic tradition that is fast vanishing.

- **The Mongols** were a people whose empire under the great Khans once spread far south into China and far west across Asia.

- **The Tatars** are six million Turkic people who now live mainly in the Tatar Republic in the Russian Federation.

# Romania and Bulgaria

- **Romania:** Capital: Bucharest. Population: 22.6 million. Currency: Leu. Language: Romanian.

- **Bulgaria:** Capital: Sofia. Population: 8.4 million. Currency: Lev. Language: Bulgarian.

- **Romania** gets its name from the Romans who occupied it almost 2,000 years ago.

- **Transylvania** is a beautiful, wooded, mountain area of Romania, once home to the 15th-century tyrant Vlad the Impaler, the original Dracula.

- **Like Bulgaria,** Romania was communist until 1989 when the people overthrew President Ceausescu.

- **Ceausescu's** attempts to develop industry forced people off the lands into towns. Many orphans were left as families broke up.

- **Romania** is a major wine grower.

- **Romania** is home not only to native Romanians but 250,000 Romanies (gypsies) who often live in caravans.

- **The Valley of Roses** is a valley near Kazanluk in Bulgaria full of fields of damask roses.

- **Bulgarian women pick** damask rose blossoms to get the oil to make 'attar of roses', used for perfumes.

◄ *Damask rose blossoms in Bulgaria's Valley of Roses are picked early mornings in May and June, before the sun dries out the petals.*

# Congo (Kinshasa)

- **Capital:** Kinshasa. Area: 2,344,880 sq km. Currency: New zaire. Language: French.
- **Physical features:** Highest mountain: Margherita Peak (5,109 m). Longest river: Congo (4,667 km).
- **Population:** 48 million. Population density: 20/sq km. Life expectancy: men 52 years; women 56 years.
- **Wealth:** GDP: $5.2 billion. GDP per head: $108.
- **Exports:** Copper, cobalt, diamonds, coffee, petroleum.
- **Congo** is called Congo (Kinshasa) or Democratic Republic of Congo to distinguish it from a neighbouring country also called

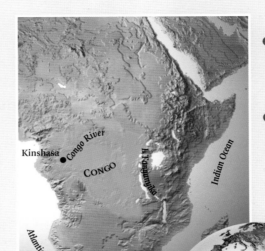

▲ Congo lies on the Equator. Over a third of it is thick equatorial rainforest.

Congo, Congo (Brazzaville).
- **From 1885 to 1971** Congo was a Belgian colony known as the Belgian Congo. From 1971 to 1997 it was called Zaire.
- **Congo** is one of the world's leading copper producers. There is a vast copper mine in Shaba (once called Katanga) in the southeast.
- **Congo is** the world's leading industrial diamonds producer.
- **The Congo River** is the world's fifth longest river, and carries more water than any river but the Amazon.

# Southern USA

- **The south central states** such as Texas, Oklahoma and New Mexico produce a lot of oil and gas.
- **Texas** produces more oil than any other state apart from Alaska.
- **Two of the world's** largest oil companies, Exxon and Amoco, were founded on Texan oil.
- **Texas** is known as the Lone Star state.

> ★ STAR FACT ★
> Dallas has the largest commercial airport in the world and the most rich people.

- **Louisiana** is known as the Sugar state because it grows so much sugar.
- **Oil wealth and aerospace** have attracted high-tech industries to Texan cities like Dallas, Houston and San Antonio.
- **Cotton** is grown on the Mississippi plains, while tobacco is important in the Carolinas and Virginia.
- **In the mid 1800s** the southern states grew 80% of the world's cotton, largely using black slave labour.
- **Florida** is famous for Disneyworld, the Cape Canaveral space centre and the Everglades, a vast area of steamy tropical swamp infested by alligators.

◄ Texas's wealth came with the discovery of oil in 1901. Now aerospace and high-tech industries are thriving in this sunny state.

# Zimbabwe

▶ *Victoria Falls on the Zambezi is one of the world's biggest waterfalls. Its roar can be heard 40 km away.*

- **Capital:** Harare. Area: 390,759 sq km. Currency: Zimbabwe dollar. Language: English.

- **Physical features:** Highest mountain: Mt Inyangani (2,595 m). Longest river: Zambezi (2,700 km).

- **Population:** 11.3 million. Population density: 28/sq km. Life expectancy: men 43.6 years; women 44.7 years.

- **Wealth:** GDP: $8.2 billion. GDP per head: $720.

- **Exports:** Cigarettes, cotton, steel, gold and nickel.

- **Zimbabwe** was once the British colony of Rhodesia but declared its independence in 1980.

- **The name Zimbabwe** came from the huge ancient stone palace of Great Zimbabwe (which means 'house of the chief').

- **Zimbabwe** is a fertile farming country, growing lots of tobacco, cotton and other crops. Much of the land still remains in the hands of white farmers, but the government plans to change this situation.

- **Zimbabwe** is the most industrial African nation after S. Africa, making steel, cement, cars, machines, textiles and much more. The industrial centre is Bulawayo.

- **98% of Zimbabweans** are black. The Shona people are the biggest group, then come the Ndebele (or Matabele). The Shona speak a language called Chishona, the Ndebele speak Sindebele.

# Chinese food

- **The staple foods** in China are rice and wheat with corn, millet and sorghum. In the south, the people eat more rice. In the north, they eat more wheat, as bread or noodles.

- **Vegetables** such as cabbage, bean and bamboo shoots are popular. So too is *tofu* (soya bean curd).

- **Favourite meats** in China are pork and poultry, but the Chinese also eat a lot of eggs, fish and shellfish.

- **A Chinese breakfast** may be rice and vegetables or rice porridge and chicken noodle soup or sweet pastries.

- **A Chinese lunch** may include egg rolls or meat or prawn dumplings called *dim sum*.

◀ *A favourite snack in China is fried savoury dumplings.*

- **A Chinese main meal** may be stir-fried vegetables with bits of meat or seafood in a stock, with rice or noodles.

- **China has** a long tradition of fine cooking, but styles vary. Cantonese cooking in the south has lots of fish, crabs and prawn. Huaiyang has steamed dishes. Szechuan is spicy. Beijing cooking in the north is the most sophisticated, famous for its Peking duck (cripsy roast duck) and Mongolian Hotpot.

- **The Chinese** often cook their food by stir-frying (stirring while hot frying) in big round pans called woks. They eat the food from bowls with chopsticks and small china spoons, not with knives and forks.

- **Chinese** drink tea without milk, typically made from jasmine leaves, oolong (green tea) or chrysanthemum.

> ★ **STAR FACT** ★
> The Chinese were drinking tea at least 4,000 years ago.

# Russia

Murmansk
St Petersburg
Barents Sea
Arctic Ocean
Kara Sea
MOSCOW
RUSSIA
Western Steppes
Caucasus Mts
Black Sea
Mt Elbrus
Caspian Sea
Volgograd
Ural Mountains
SIBERIA
Omsk
Sayan Mountains
Eastern Steppes
Irkutsk
Lake Baikal
Sea of Okhotsk
KAMCHATKA
Vladivostok

In eastern Siberia, milk is sold in frozen blocks with a wooden handle

Lake Baikal is the world's oldest and deepest lake

Vladivostok is the terminus of the 9,300 km Trans-Siberian Railway, the world's longest railway

▶ Russia stretches 10,000 km – almost a third of the way around the world – from the open steppes south of Moscow to the chilly pine forests of the Kamchatka in the east.

- **Capital:** Moscow. Area: 17,075,400 sq km. Currency: Rouble. Language: Russian.

- **Physical features:** Highest mountain: Mt Elbrus (5,642 m). Longest river: the Ob-Irtysh (5,411 km).

- **Population:** 147.7 million. Population density: 9/sq km. Life expectancy: men 60.6 years; women 72.8 years.

- **Wealth:** GDP: $394.9 billion. GDP per head: $2,680. Exports: chemicals, machinery, minerals, natural gas, paper products, petroleum, wood products.

- **Russia** or the Russian Federation is the country created by the Russians after the break up of the Soviet Union in 1991. It includes republics such as Chechnya, Osetiya, Kalmykiya, Tatarstan, Mordoviya and Bashkortostan. Many of these republics, such as Chechnya, are waiting to be independent.

▼ The Ural mountains run from north to south forming a natural boundary between Russia and Siberia, Europe and Asia.

- **Russia is** the biggest country in the world, almost twice as big as the next country, Canada. It stretches from the subtropical south to the Arctic north, where it has the longest Arctic coastline of any country.

- **Russia has huge** mineral resources and is among the world's leading producers of oil, natural gas, coal, asbestos, manganese, silver, tin and zinc. It also has giant forests for timber in the east in Siberia.

- **Russia** has some of the biggest factories in the world around Moscow, producing everything from high-tech goods to iron and steel and trucks. Yet in the far north and east, people still live as they have done for many thousands of years, herding reindeer or hunting.

- **After the USSR broke up**, Russia and its people were plunged into crisis. Encouraged by western nations, Russian presidents – first Boris Yeltsin, then Vladimir Putin – have tried to establish a free market economy in place of the old communist one.

★ STAR FACT ★
In Yakutsk in Siberia, winter temperatures can plunge to -69°C while summers can soar to 39°C – more extreme than anywhere else. Oymako is the world's coldest town. It once had temperatures of -72°C.

# New Zealand

 *New Zealand is made up of two islands – the almost sub-tropical North island where most people live and the long, narrow South island with its wide Canterbury Plains and soaring Southern Alps.*

- **Capital:** Wellington. Area: 270,534 sq km. Currency: NZ dollar. Language: English.

- **Physical features:** Highest mountain: Mt Cook (3,764 m). Longest river: Waikato (425 km).

- **Population:** 3.8 million. Population density: 14/sq km. Life expectancy: men 74.1 years; women 79.7 years.

- **Wealth:** GDP: $59.5 billion. GDP per head: $15,830.

- **Exports:** Meat, milk, butter, cheese, wool, fish, fruit.

- **New Zealand** was one of the last places to be inhabited by humans and remains a clean, beautiful land, with rolling farmland, thick forests and towering mountains.

- **New Zealand** is mainly a farming country, with over 50% of the land devoted to crops and pasture for sheep and cattle. 75% of New Zealand's exports are farm produce.

- **Fast-flowing** rivers provide 75% of New Zealand's power through hydroelectric plants. Geothermal energy from hot springs provides some of the rest. Nuclear power is banned.

- **The first** inhabitants of New Zealand were the Maoris, who came about AD800 and now form 13% of the population. The remaining 87% are mostly descended from British settlers who came in the 19th and 20th centuries.

> ★ **STAR FACT** ★
> There are 70 million sheep in New Zealand – 20 sheep to every person!

# Yellowstone Park

- **Yellowstone** is the oldest and best-known national park in the USA. It was established by Act of Congress on March 1, 1872.

- **It is one of the world's largest** parks covering 8,983 sq km of rugged mountains and spectacular deep valleys.

- **It is situated** across Wyoming, Montana and Idaho.

- **Yellowstone** is famous for its lakes and rivers such Yellowstone Lake and Snake River.

- **Most of Yellowstone** is forested in lodgepole pines, along with other conifers, cottonwoods and aspens. It also has a wealth of wild flowers.

▼ *Yellowstone sits on top of a volcanic hot spot which gives it its famous geysers and hot springs – and may make it the site of the biggest eruption of all time.*

- **Yellowstone's** wild animals include bison, elk, bighorn sheep, moose, grizzly bears and wolves.

- **Yellowstone** has the world's greatest concentration of geothermal features including 10,000 hot springs and 200 geysers, as well as steam vents, mud cauldrons, fumaroles and paint pots.

- **The most famous geyser** is Old Faithful, which spouts every hour or so. The biggest is the 115 m Steamboat.

- **One of the biggest** volcanic eruptions ever occured in Yellowstone Park two million years ago. Enough lava poured out in one go to build six Mt Fujiyamas.

- **There are signs** that Yellowstone may soon erupt as a 'supervolcano' – an eruption on an unimaginable scale.

# International organizations

◄ *The Red Cross was set up by Swiss Jean Dunant in the 19th century after he witnessed the bloody slaughter at the battle of Solferino in Italy. It now plays a vital role in helping suffering people everywhere.*

- **International organizations** are of three main types: those set up by governments, like the UN; multinationals; and human rights and welfare organizations like the Red Cross and Amnesty International.

- **The United Nations** or UN was formed after World War II to maintain world peace and security. It now has over 160 member nations.

- **UN headquarters** are in New York City. The name was coined by US President Roosevelt in 1941.

- **All UN members** meet in the General Assembly. It has five permanent members (Russia, USA, China, France and UK) and ten chosen every two years.

- **The UN** has agencies responsible for certain areas such as children (UNICEF), food and farming (FAO), health (WHO), science (UNESCO) and nuclear energy (IAEA).

- **Multinationals** or TNCs (transnational corporations) are huge companies that work in many countries.

- **TNCs** like Coca-Cola and Kodak are well known; others like cigarette-makers Philip Morris are less known.

- **Some TNCs** take in more money than most countries. Just 500 TNCs control 70% of all the world's trade.

- **90% of world** grain is handled by six big US TNCs. Cargill and Continental alone control half the world's grain.

- **Amnesty International** was founded in 1961 to campaign for those imprisoned for religious and political beliefs.

# Italy

- **Capital:** Rome. Area 301,245 sq km. Currency: Lira. Language: Italian.

- **Physical features:** Highest mountain: Monte Rosa (4,638 m). Longest river: Po (652 km).

- **Population:** 57.4 million. Population density: 190/sq km. Life expectancy: men 75 years; women 81.2.

- **Wealth:** GDP: $1,160 billion. GDP per head: $20,100.

- **Exports:** Wine, machinery, cars and trucks, footwear, clothes, olive oil, textiles, mineral products.

- **Italy** is a narrow, mountainous country. The north is cool and moist, with big industrial cities. Tuscany and Umbria have rich farmland and ancient cities famous for their art treasures. The south is hot, dusty and often poor.

- **Vines and olives** are grown widely and Italy is one of the world's main producers of both wine and olive oil.

- **Italy is one of the biggest** industrial nations. Industry is concentrated in the north in cities like Turin and Milan. Here they make cars, computers, chemicals and textiles.

▲ *The ancient city of Venice is set on 117 islands in a lagoon. Instead of streets, there are 177 canals, plied by boats called gondolas.*

- **Italians** like to dress in style and the fashion trade is big business. Italian fashion labels like Armani, Versace, Valentino, Moschino and Gucci are now world famous.

- **Italy is full of beautiful** historic towns like Florence, Padua and Mantua, many dating from the Renaissance.

# Rich and poor

Above $15,000
$10,000–15,000
$5,000–10,000

$1,000–5,000
$ Below 1,000
Not known

▶ One of the clearest ways of seeing the huge gap in wealth between countries is by looking at the gross domestic product (GDP) per head. This is what a person would get if the country's entire income was split up equally among everyone. This map shows the GDP per head for all the world's countries.

★ STAR FACT ★
About half a billion people are starving or don't get enough to eat.

- **The world's richest country** is the USA, with a GDP of $7,783 billion. But people in Switzerland have an even higher GDP per head – $43,060.

- **The world's poorest country** by GDP per head is Burma (Myanmar). Each person has, on average, $100, but many are even poorer.

- **The world's richest countries** with less than a quarter of the world's population take three-quarters of its wealth.

- **Most of the world's rich countries** are in the Northern Hemisphere. Most poor countries are in the South. So people talk of the North-South divide.

- **One billion people** around the world live in 'absolute poverty'. This means they have no real homes. In cities, they sleep rough or live in shacks. They rarely have enough to eat or drink.

- **In the 1970s** richer countries encouraged poorer countries like Mexico and Brazil to borrow money to build new dams and industrial works.

- **By 1999** poor countries were paying $50 billion more in debt interest than rich countries were donating in aid.

- **Famine** has become a common problem in the poorer parts of the world. One reason is that so much farmland is used for growing crops for export – raising the cost of food, and restricting the land available for growing food for local people.

- **250,000** children die a week from a poor diet. 250,000 die a month from diarrhoea, because of a lack of clean water.

◀ Since 1960, the divide between North and South has grown wider leaving many in abject poverty.

# Israel

- **Capital:** Jerusalem. Area: 20,770 sq km. Currency: New Shekel. Languages: Hebrew, Arabic.
- **Physical features:** Highest mountain: Mt Meron (1,208 m). Longest river: River Jordan (359 km).
- **Population:** 5.9 million. Population density: 264/sq km. Life expectancy: men 75.7 years; women 79.7 years.
- **Wealth:** GDP: $94.4 billion. GDP per head: $16,180.
- **Exports:** Fruit and vegetables, chemical products, oil products, diamonds, textiles, machinery, fertilizers.
- **Israel** was founded in 1948 as a home for Jews who have since come here from all over the world.
- **The city of Jericho** may be the oldest in the world, dating back more than 10,000 years.

> ★ **STAR FACT** ★
> Jerusalem is sacred for three major religions: Judaism, Islam and Christianity.

- **Many people** in rural areas work on kibbutzim – collective farms where work and profits are shared.
- **Israel is famous** for its Jaffa oranges, named after Jaffa, the old name for the city of Tel Aviv. They are grown on the Plain of Sharon.

# Rome

- **Rome** is the capital of Italy, and its biggest city, with a population of almost three million.
- **Rome's Vatican** is the home of the Pope.
- **The Vatican** is the smallest independent country in the world covering just 0.4 sq km.
- **Rome is known** as the eternal city because of its long and dramatic history.
- **Ancient Rome ruled** much of Europe and the lands around the Mediterranean for hundreds of years as the capital of the Roman Empire.
- **Ancient Rome** was famously built on seven hills – the Aventine, Caelian, Capitoline, Esquiline, Palatine, Quirinal and Viminal.
- **Rome has** one of the richest collections of art treasures and historic buildings in the world. The Trevi is one of many beautiful fountains.
- **There are many Ancient Roman** relics in Rome including the Colosseum arena and the Pantheon.

▲ St Peter's Church is located in the Vatican city in Rome. It is the largest church in the world.

- **The Vatican's** Sistine Chapel has a ceiling painted brilliantly by Michelangelo and frescoes (wall paintings) by Botticelli, Ghirlandaio and Perugino.
- **Rome is** now a major centre for film-making, publishing and tourism.

# Peoples of Africa

- **Africa has been** inhabited longer than any other continent. The earliest human fossils were found here.

- **In the north** in countries such as Algeria, Morocco and Egypt, people are mainly Arabic.

- **The Berber people** were the first people to live in northwest Africa, with a culture dating back to at least 2400BC. Their culture survives in remote villages in the Atlas mountains of Algeria and Morocco.

- **Tuaregs** are camel-herding nomads who live in the Sahara desert, but much of their traditional grazing land has been taken over by permanent farms.

- **South of the Sahara** most people are black Africans.

- ◀ *Zulus are Bantu-speaking people who live in South Africa. They have a proud warrior tradition.*

- **There are more than 800** ethnic groups of black Africans.

- **Over 1,300** different languages are spoken in Africa, more than any other continent.

- **Most people** in southern Africa speak English or one of 100 Bantu languages such as Zulu or Swahili.

- **Many people** in rural southern Africa live in round houses.

- **Africa was ruled** by the Europeans as colonies. By the early 20th century the country was divided into nations. Many small groups became dominated by tribes and cultures perhaps hostile to their own.

# Turkey and Cyprus

- **Turkey:** Capital: Ankara. Population: 63.4 million. Currency: Turkish Lira. Language: Turkish.

- **Cyprus:** Capital: Nicosia. Population: 708,000. Currency: Cyprus pound. Languages: Greek and Turkish.

- **Turkey lies** partly in Europe, partly in Asia. The two continents are separated by a narrow sea called the Bosphorus.

- ◀ *A hubble-bubble is a special pipe popular in Turkey. Sucking on the long pipe draws the smoke bubbling through water.*

- **Turkey is a republic** with a mix of Islamic and Western traditions.

- **Istanbul** is one of the world's great historic capital cities. As Byzantium, it was capital of the Byzantine Empire for 1,000 years. Then it was Constantinople, the capital of the great Ottoman Empire for 500 years, until 1920.

- **Street cafés** are popular with Turkish men, who come to drink thick, dark, sweet Turkish coffee, smoke pipes called hubble-bubbles and play backgammon.

- **25 million Kurds** live on the borders of Turkey, Iran, Iraq and Syria and have no country of their own.

- **31% Turkish people** live in the country growing wheat, cotton, tobacco, sugar beet, fruit and tea.

- **Turkey's national motto** is *Yurtta sulh, Cihand sulh* ('Peace at home, peace in the world').

- **Turkish food** is famous for its *shish kebabs* – cubes of meat and vegetables barbecued on a skewer.

# Venezuela & neighbours

▲ Venezuela and its neighbours lie along the northern coast of South America, along the edge of the tropical waters of the Caribbean.

- **Venezuela:** Capital: Caracas. Population: 22.8 million. Currency: Bolivar. Language: Spanish.

- **Colombia:** Capital: Bogota. Population: 40 million. Currency: Colombian peso. Language: Spanish.

- **Guyana:** Capital: Georgetown. Population: 825,000. Currency: Guyana dollar. Language: English.

- **Surinam:** Capital: Paramaribo. Population: 425,000. Currency: Surinam guilder. Language: Dutch.

- **French Guiana:** Capital: Cayenne. Population: 114,000. Currency: French franc. Language: French.

- **The discovery of oil** in Venezuela's Lake Maracaibo in 1917 turned it from one of South America's poorest countries to one of its richest.

- **The Venezuelan city** of Merida has the world's highest cable car, going up 4,765 m.

- **The world's highest waterfall** is the Angel Falls in Venezuela, plunging 980 m.

- **The Yanomami** are native peoples who survive in remote forest regions of Venezuela and live by hunting with spears and gathering roots and fruit.

- **Kourou** in French Guiana is the launch site for European spacecraft such as the Ariane.

# New York

> ★ **STAR FACT** ★
> New York is the USA's largest port, its trade centre and the finance centre of the world.

- **New York City** is the largest city in the USA and one of the largest in the world, with a population of 7.5 million.

- **Over 18 million people** live in the New York metropolitan area.

- **New York has five** main boroughs: Manhattan, Brooklyn, the Bronx, Queens and Staten Island.

- **Manhattan** is the oldest part of the city, but now has its tallest skyscrapers, including the Empire State Building (1931), for 40 years the world's tallest building at 381 m.

- **The 411 m high** World Trade Center is one of the world's tallest buildings.

- **New York's most famous** statue is the Statue of Liberty, erected in 1886 at the entrance to New York harbour.

- **Dutch settler** Peter Minuit is said to have bought Manhattan island from the Iroquois Indians for $24.

- **New York** began in 1625 as the Dutch settlement of New Amsterdam. It was renamed New York when the English took over in 1664.

- **New York's famous** finance centre Wall Street is named after a protective wall built by Dutch colonists in 1653.

▼ The skyscrapers of Manhattan give New York one of the most famous skylines in the world.

# Population

- **The world's population** climbed above 6 billion in 1999.
- **Over a quarter** of a million babies are born every day around the world.
- **World population** is growing at a rate of about 1.6% per year.
- **At the current rate** world population will hit 10 billion by 2020.
- **Between 1950** and 1990, the world's population doubled from about 2.5 billion to 5 billion, adding 2.5 billion people in 40 years.
- **The 1990s** added a billion people. The next decade will add 1.5 billion. This adds 2.5 billion in 20 years.

Asia: 63%

Australasia: 0.5%

Africa: 12.5%

Europe: 10.4 %

Antarctica: 0%

North America: 6.9%

South America: 6.7%

◀ People are not spread evenly around the world. Some continents, like Europe, are densely populated. Antarctica is empty. The size of the figures in this diagram shows the size of the population of each continent. The size of the segment the figure is standing on shows the area of the continent.

- **Asia has** about 60% of the world's population. China alone has 1.3 billion people and India has 1 billion.
- **The number of babies** born to each woman varies from 1.15 in Spain to 7.6 in Yemen.
- **Latvia** has 100 women to every 85.3 men; Qatar has 197.8 men every 100 women.
- **In the developed world** people are living longer. In Japan people expect to live 80 years on average. In Sierra Leone, people only live 37.2 years.

# Berlin

- **Berlin** is Germany's capital and largest city, with a population of about 3.5 million.
- **Berlin** was originally capital of Prussia, which expanded to become Germany in the 1800s.
- **The city** was wrecked by Allied bombs in World War II.
- **After the War** Berlin was left inside the new communist East Germany and split into East and West by a high wall.

> ★ STAR FACT ★
> Almost every Berliner has a fragment of the Wall, torn down in 1989.

- **East Berlin** was the capital of East Germany; the West German capital moved to Bonn.
- **In 1989** the East German government collapsed and the Berlin Wall was torn down. East and West Germany were united in 1990 and Berlin was made capital again.
- **The Brandenburg Gate** is a huge stone arch built in 1791. It now marks the boundary between east and west.
- **Kurfurstendamm** is a famous shopping avenue. The Hansa quarter was designed by architects in the 1950s.
- **Since reunification** many spectacular new buildings have been built in Berlin including the refurbished Reichstag designed by Norman Foster.

◀ When Germany was reunited, the old Reichstag became home of the German parliament again. It has now been given a major facelift.

# The USA

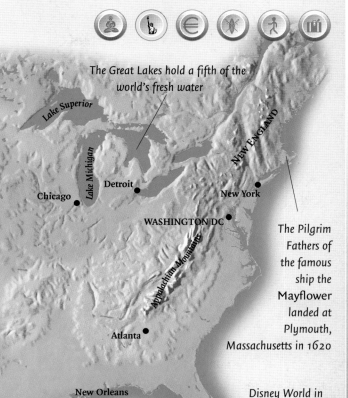

The Great Lakes hold a fifth of the world's fresh water

Lake Superior

Seattle

Cascade Range

Coast Ranges

Rocky Mountains

NEW ENGLAND

Lake Michigan

Detroit

Chicago

New York

San Francisco

Great Basin

CALIFORNIA

WASHINGTON DC

Appalachian Mountains

Grand Canyon

Los Angeles

Atlanta

The Pilgrim Fathers of the famous ship the Mayflower landed at Plymouth, Massachusetts in 1620

Houston

New Orleans

FLORIDA

Miami

Disney World in Orlando, Florida, is one of the world's biggest theme parks

Where it flows into the Gulf of Mexico, North America's longest river the Mississippi creates a huge delta

▶ The United States is the richest and most powerful country in the world. Nearly 280 million people live here, and it covers a vast area of North America, from the freezing wastes of Alaska to the hot and steamy Everglades (marshes) of Florida.

- **Capital:** Washington DC. Area: 9,372,610 sq km. Currency: US dollar. Language: English.

- **Physical features:** Highest mountain: Mt McKinley (6,194 m). Longest river: the Mississippi-Missouri-Red Rock (6,019 km).

- **Population:** 278.1 million. Population density: 29/sq km. Life expectancy: men 73.4 years; women 80.1 years.

- **Wealth:** GDP: $7,783 billion. GDP per head: $29,080.

- **Exports:** Aircraft, vehicles, chemicals, machinery, electronic goods, coal, oil, maize, wheat, soya beans.

- **Native Americans lived** in North America for 10,000 years before the Europeans arrived in the 16th century and gradually drove westwards, brushing the Native Americans aside. In 1788, English colonists founded the United States of America, now the world's oldest democratic republic, with a famous constitution (set of laws).

- **The USA** is the world's fourth largest in area, third largest in population, and has the largest GDP.

- **In the 1950s and 60s** Americans earned more money, ate more food, used more energy and drove more cars than anyone else in the world.

> ★ **STAR FACT** ★
> One in two Americans owns a computer – more than any other country in the world.

- **Now the USA** is the world's prime consumer of energy, oil, copper, lead, zinc, aluminium, corn, coffee and cocoa. It is also prime producer of aluminium and corn, and one of the top five producers of energy, oil, copper, lead, zinc, wheat and sugar.

▼ Through the films made in Hollywood, California, most of the world has become familiar with the American 'dream' of success.

# Moscow and St Petersburg

▲ St Petersburg is an elegant city with many beautiful houses and palaces such as the famous Hermitage museum.

- **Moscow** is the largest city in the Russian Federation and capital of Russia.

- **Moscow** is Russia's main industrial centre, with huge textile and car-making plants, like the Likhachyov works.

- **Moscow's biggest shops** are Detsky Mir (Children's World) and GUM, the government store on Red Square.

- **Moscow's historic centre** is Red Square and the Kremlin, the walled city-within-a-city.

- **In the past** Moscow had wooden buildings and was often burnt down, most famously by Napoleon's troops in 1812.

- **Moscow is snow-covered** from November to April each year, but snow-ploughs keep all the main roads clear.

- **St Petersburg** is Russia's second largest city.

- **St Petersburg** was founded in 1703 by Tsar Peter the Great to be his capital instead of Moscow.

- **After the 1917 Russian Revolution**, communists called Petersburg (then called Petrograd) Leningrad and made Moscow capital. St Petersburg regained its name in 1991.

# India

- **Capital:** New Delhi. Area: 3,287,263 sq km. Currency: Indian rupee. Languages: Hindi and English.

- **Physical features:** Highest mountain: Kanchenjunga (8,598 m). Longest river: Ganges (2,510 km).

▼ Hindu women in India traditionally wear beautifully coloured wraps or saris made of fine cloth such as silk.

- **Population:** 1 billion. Population density: 284/sq km. Life expectancy: men 62.3 years; women 62.9 years.

- **Wealth:** GDP: $357.4 billion. GDP per head: $370.

- **Exports:** Gems, jewellery, clothes, cotton, textiles, tea, engineering goods.

- **India has heavy** monsoon rains for six months of the year and dry weather for the rest.

- **India is the world's** largest democracy.

- **Two-thirds** of India's population grow their own food, mainly rice and wheat.

- **India's wheat production** has doubled since the Green Revolution of the 1960s when high-yield hybrids were introduced – but much wheat is sold abroad, pushing prices too high for many poor Indians.

- **India is the world's** 10th biggest industrial nation. Textiles remain important, but there is a growing emphasis on heavy industry, including iron and steel, vehicles, machine tools and pharmaceuticals.

# Brazil

- **Capital:** Brasilia. Area: 8,512,000 sq km. Currency: Real. Language: Portuguese.

- **Physical features:** Highest mountain: Neblina (3,014 m). Longest river: the Amazon (6,439 km).

- **Population:** 163.7 million. Population density: 19/sq km. Life expectancy: men 63.1 years; women 71 years.

- **Wealth:** GDP: $820 billion. GDP per head: $4,790.

- **Exports:** Iron ore, coffee, fruit, timber, sugar, vehicles, beef.

- **Brazil has the biggest** national debt of any country in the world – not far short of $200 billion.

*Atlantic Ocean*
*Amazon River*
*Andes Mts*
*BRAZIL*
*Rio de Janeiro*
*Sao Paulo*
*Rio de la Plata*

- ◀ Brazil is the world's fifth largest country, but most people live on the eastern edge. Much of the central area is cerrado (grass wilderness) or thick Amazon rainforest.

- **Brazil** is the world's biggest coffee grower. Soya, sugarcane, cotton, oranges, bananas and cocoa are also major crops.

- **The city of São Paulo** has grown faster than any other big city in the world and now 17 million people live there. Housing shortages in cities such as Rio de Janeiro and São Paulo mean 25 million Brazilians live in rickety sheds in sprawling shanty towns called *favelas*.

- **Brazilians are soccer-mad** and have won the World Cup more times than any other country.

- **The Amazon basin** contains the world's largest area of virgin rainforest – but an area almost the size of Ireland is being cleared each year for short-term cattle ranching.

# North European food

J127,889

- **Fish and bread** play a major role in the traditional Scandinavian diet.

- **Gravadlax** is a Swedish form of smoked salmon, usually served with pepper, dill and mustard sauce.

- **Smörgåsbord** is a Swedish speciality. It is a huge spread of bread and cold foods, including fish such as herring and salmon, and also cheeses.

- **Smörgåsbord** gets its name from the Swedish *smörgås*, meaning bread and *bord*, meaning table.

- **Every region in Germany** has its own range of foods, but things like *wurst* (sausages), pretzels and *sauerkraut* (pickled cabbage) are widely popular.

- **The German national drink** is beer, and every October a huge beer festival is held in Munich.

- **England is well known** for its hearty stews and winter roasts, especially roast beef. But the most popular food for those eating out is Indian.

- **An English speciality** is fish (deep-fried in batter) and chips (fried slices of potato).

- **Vienna** in Austria is renowned for its coffee houses where the Viennese sit and eat *Kaffee und Kuchen* (coffee and cakes).

- **Poland is famous** for its rye bread and thick beet.

- ▼ The seas around Northern Europe were once teeming with fish and fish still plays a major role in the diet of people here.

# Japan

- **Capital:** Tokyo. Area: 377,727 sq km. Currency: Yen. Language: Japanese.

- **Physical features:** Highest mountain: Mt Fujiyama (3,776 m). Longest river: the Shinano-gawa (370 km).

- **Population:** 126 million. Population density: 332/sq km. Life expectancy: Men 76.8 years; women 82.9 years.

- **Wealth:** GDP: $4,812.1 billion. GDP per head: $38,160.

- **Exports:** Electronic goods, steel, cars, ships, chemicals, textiles, machinery.

- **Japan** is very mountainous, so the big cities where nine out of ten people live are crowded into the coastal plains. 40 million people are crammed into Tokyo and its suburbs alone, making it the biggest urban centre in the world. Tokyo and the nearby cities have tall skyscrapers to make the most of the limited space available – but also with deep foundations, because Japan is prone to earthquakes.

- **Japan** is famous for its electronic goods – including walkmans and games consoles. It also makes huge amounts of steel, half the world's ships and more cars than any other country.

The Seikan Tunnel links Hokkaido to Honshu under the stormy Tsugaru Straits

The Hida, Japan's highest mountains, are also known as the Japanese Alps

◄ Japan is made up of four large islands – Hokkaido, Honshu, Shikoku and Kyushu – and nearly 4,000 smaller ones, stretching over almost 2,000 km of the western Pacific Ocean. 75% of Japanese people live on Honshu, the largest island. But the most densely populated is Kyushu. After some gigantic engineering projects in the late 20th century, Kyushu, Honshu, Shikoku and other islands are now all linked by bridges and tunnels. The massive Seto Ohashi bridge links several islands. The bridge from Honshu to Shikoku at Akashi-Kaikyo has the world's longest single span – 2 km. Hokkaido and Honshu are linked by the Seikan tunnel, the world's longest undersea tunnel, 53.85 km long.

- **All but 15%** of the land is too steep for farming, but millions of little square rice fields are packed on to the coastal plains and on hillside terraces.

- **Most Japanese live** a very modern way of life. But traditions still survive and there are many ancient Buddhist and Shinto shrines.

▼ The beautiful, snow-capped Mt Fujiyama is the most famous of Japan's 2,000 volcanoes and is sacred to the Shinto religion.

> ★ STAR FACT ★
> Japan has the world's largest fishing industry with 400,000 vessels catching 12 million tonnes of fish a year.

# Australian landmarks

- **Australia's most famous landmark** is Uluru or Ayers Rock, the biggest monolith (single block of stone) in the world, 348 m high and 9 km around.

- **Uluru** is the tip of a huge bed of coarse sand laid down in an inland sea some 600 million years ago.

- **Lake Eyre** is Australia's lowest point, 15 m below sea level. It is also Australia's biggest lake by far, but it is normally dry and fills only once every 50 years or so.

- **Nullarbor plain** is a vast, dry plain in southern Australia. Its name comes from the Latin *nulla arbor* ('no tree').

- **Shark Bay** is famous for its sharks and dolphins.

- **Shark Bay** is also famous for its stromatolites, the world's oldest fossils, dating back 3.5 billion years. These are pizza-like mats made by colonies of blue-green algae.

> ★ STAR FACT ★
> The Great Barrier Reef is the world's largest
> structure made by living things.

▲ *Uluru is sacred to the Aboriginals. On its surface and in its caves are paintings made long ago by Aboriginal artists.*

- **The Darling River** is Australia's longest river (2,739 km long), but it only flows in summer.

- **The Great Barrier Reef** is a coral reef off the coast of Queensland in northwest Australia.

- **The Great Barrier Reef** is the world's biggest coral reef, over 2,000 km long.

# Ukraine and Belarus

- **Ukraine:** Capital: Kiev. Population: 51.3 million. Currency: Hryvnya. Language: Ukrainian.

- **Belarus:** Capital: Minsk. Population: 10.4 million. Currency: Belarusian rouble. Language: Belarussian.

- **Ukraine** is Europe's largest country (except for Russia), covering over 600,000 sq km.

- **Ukraine** is famous for its vast plains or *steppes*. The fertile black soils have made it 'the breadbasket of Europe', growing huge amounts of wheat and barley.

- **During the Soviet era** Soviet policies forced Ukrainians to speak Russian and adopt Russian culture, but the Ukrainian identity has been found again since they gained independence in 1991.

▶ *Ukraine and Belarus are flat countries that form the western margin of Russia, north of the Black Sea.*

- **In the Soviet era** over a quarter of Ukraine's industrial output was arms. Now Ukraine is trying to use these factories to make other products.

- **In 1986** a terrible accident occurred at the Chernobyl nuclear power plant north of Kiev. A reactor exploded spreading radioactovity over a wide area.

- **Nuclear energy** still provides 25% of Ukraine's power, but many Ukrainians are firmly against it.

- **Belarus** (known as Byelorussia under the USSR) is a flat country, covered in many places by thick forests and marshes. The Pripet Marshes are the largest in Europe covering 27,000 sq km.

- **Belarus** is known for making heavy-duty trucks, tractors and bicycles among other things. The forests provide products such as furniture, matches and paper.

# Peoples of Australia

- **The Aborigines** make up 1.5 % of Australia's population today, but they were the first inhabitants.

- **The word aborigine** comes from the Latin *ab origine*, which means 'from the start'.

- **Aborigine cave paintings** and tools have been found in Australia dating back to at least 45,000 years ago.

- **Aborigines** prefer to be called Kooris.

- **British people** began to settle in Australia about 200 years ago. They now form the majority of the population, along with other white Europeans.

- **Many of the earliest** settlers in Australia were convicts, transported from Britain for minor crimes.

◀ *The Kooris or Aborigines of Australia spread right across the Pacific many thousands of years ago and were probably the first inhabitants of America as well.*

- **Many Australians** have ancestral roots in the British Isles.

- **The British settlers** drove the Aborigines from their land and 60% now live in cities.

- **After hard campaigning** some Aboriginal sacred sites are being returned to them, with their original names. Ayers Rock is now known as Uluru. A famous trial in 1992 returned to Aborigine Eddy Mabo land on Murray Island first occupied by his ancestors before the Europeans arrived.

- **Many recent immigrants** to Australia are from Southeast Asia and Greece.

# Kazakhstan & neighbours

- **Kazakhstan:** Capital: Akmola. Population: 16.37 million. Currency: Tenge. Language: Kazakh.

- **Uzbekistan:** Capital: Tashkent. Population: 24.1 million. Currency: Som. Language: Uzbek.

- **Turkmenistan:** Capital: Ashkabad. Population: 4.7 million. Currency: Manat. Language: Turkmen.

- **Many of the people** in this part of the world are still nomads, moving from place to place in search of new pastures for their herds.

- **Uzbekistan** has become wealthy from natural gas

◀ *The break-up of the Soviet Union left the countries around the Caspian Sea a legacy of some of the world's worst pollution. But they have a wealth of minerals and a venerable history.*

> ★ **STAR FACT** ★
> Kazakhstan has huge iron and coal reserves and the world's largest chrome mine.

and also from cotton, which they call 'white gold'.

- **The Baykonur Cosmodrome** in Kazakhstan is where the Russians launch most of their spacecraft.

- **The Soviet Union** forced nomads in Kalmykiya by the Caspian Sea to boost sheep production beyond what the fragile steppe grass could handle. This created 1.4 million acres of desert.

- **The Aral Sea** on the Kazakh/Uzbek border was once the world's fourth largest lake. But irrigating farmland has cut the supply of water from the Amu Darya River and the Aral Sea is now shrinking rapidly.

- **The Caspian Sea** once had the sturgeon fish giving the most highly prized beluga caviar, but pollution has decimated the fish population.

# East Africa

▲ *Tanzania is famous for safaris in the Serengeti park where lions, elephants, giraffes and many other animals are seen.*

Currency: Franc. Languages: French and Kurundi.

- **Uganda:** Capital: Kampala. Population: 20.6 million. Currency: Shilling. Language: English.

- **Malawi:** Capital: Lilongwe. Population: 11.1 million. Currency: Kwacha. Languages: Chewa and English.

- **A fifth of Malawi** is taken up by Lake Nyasa, one of the world's largest, deepest lakes and home to the usipa, a sardine-like fish that in dried form provides the people of Malawi with their main protein.

- **The countries** of East Africa are the least urbanized in the world with 9 out of 10 living in the countryside.

- **In 1994** Rwanda and Burundi were ravaged by the worst genocide in African history as tribal war flared between the Tutsi and Hutu peoples.

- **Lake Victoria** on the Tanzania and Uganda border covers 69.484 sq km, one of the world's largest lakes.

- **One of Tanzania's** main crops is sisal, a kind of palm. Sisal leaves are crushed to extract fibre to make rope.

- **Tanzania:** Capital: Dodoma. Population: 28.8 million. Currency: Shilling. Languages: English and Swahili.

- **Rwanda:** Capital: Kigali. Population: 7.7 million. Currency: Franc. Languages: French and Kinyarwanda.

- **Burundi:** Capital: Bujumbura. Population: 6 million.

# The Gran Chaco

- **The Gran Chaco** is a vast area of tropical grassland in Argentina, Paraguay and Bolivia.

- **It covers** an area of over 750 million sq km, an area as large as northwest Europe.

- **It is home** to scattered native Indian groups such as the Gaicurú, Lengua, Mataco, Vilela, Zamuco and Tupi people.

- **The word Chaco** comes from the Quechua Indian word for 'Hunting Land' because it is rich in wildlife. *Gran* is Spanish for 'big'.

- **The major activities** on the Chaco are cattle grazing and cotton growing.

- **In the east** huge factories have been built to process tannin from the trees for leather production.

- **In places** grass can grow up to 3 m tall, higher than a rider on horseback.

- **The Chaco** is home to many wild animals, including pumas, tapir, giant rheas and giant armadillos.

- **The Chaco** is the last refuge of the South American maned or red wolf.

▶ *The jaguar is the Chaco's biggest hunting animal, and the biggest cat in the Americas. Yet unlike other big cats, it never roars. It just makes a strange cry rather like a loud sneeze.*

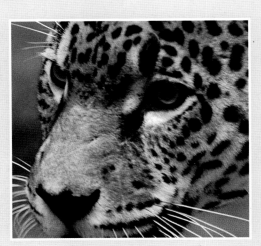

> ★ **STAR FACT** ★
> The sediments under the Gran Chaco are well over 3,000 m deep in places.

# Poland and neighbours

▲ Poland and its neighbours cluster around the Baltic Sea.

- **Poland:** Capital: Warsaw. Population: 38.7 million. Currency: Zloty. Language: Polish.
- **Lithuania:** Capital: Vilnius. Population: 3.7 million. Currency: Litas. Language: Lithuanian.
- **Latvia:** Capital: Riga. Population: 2.5 million. Currency: Lats. Language: Latvian.

- **Estonia:** Capital: Tallinn. Population: 1.4 million. Currency: Kroon. Language: Estonian.
- **Poland** was led away from communism by trade union leader Lech Walesa, who became the first president of democratic Poland in 1990.
- **The name Poland** comes from the Slavic word *polane* which means plain, and much of Poland is flat plains.
- **The shipyards at Gdansk** on the Baltic make Poland the world's fifth largest builder of merchant ships.
- **Krakow** has many historic buildings but the nearby Nowa Huta steelworks make it very polluted.
- **Latvia, Lithuania** and Estonia are Catholic countries. Their way of life suffered in the Soviet era. They are now rebuilding their identity.
- **Latvian** is one of the oldest European languages, related to the ancient Indian language Sanskrit.

# West Coast USA

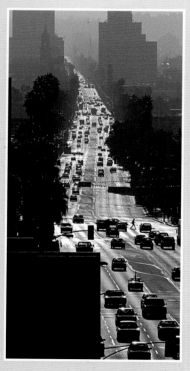

- **The western USA is** mountainous, with peaks in the Rockies, Cascades and Sierra Nevada soaring over 4,000 m.
- **Seattle** is the home of computer software giant Microsoft, and Boeing, the world's biggest aircraft maker.
- **Seattle** is the home of the Starbucks café chain – made famous by the TV series *Frasier*.

◀ Sunset Boulevard in LA is a 30 km long road. Its Sunset Strip section is popular with film stars.

- **Los Angeles** (LA) sprawls over a larger area than any other city in the world and has endless kilometres of freeways.
- **Film-makers** came to the LA suburb of Hollywood in 1907 because of California's sunshine. It has been the world's greatest film-making centre ever since.
- **The San Andreas fault** is the boundary between two huge continental plates. As it moves it gives west coast cities earthquakes. The worst may be yet to come.
- **San Francisco's** Golden Gate is named after the 1849 rush when prospectors came in thousands to look for gold.
- **California is** known as the 'Sunshine State'.
- **California's** San Joaquin valley is one of the world's major wine-growing regions.

> ★ STAR FACT ★
> Silicon Valley near San Francisco has the world's greatest concentration of electronics firms.

# World religions

- **Christianity** is the world's largest religion, with 1.5 billion followers worldwide. Christians believe in a saviour, Jesus Christ, a Jew who lived in Israel 2,000 years ago. Christ, they believe, was the Son of God. When crucified to death (nailed to a wooden cross), he rose from the dead to join God in heaven.

- **Islam** is the world's second largest religion with 1.3 billion believers. It was founded in Arabia in the 7th century by Mohammed, who Muslims believe was the last, greatest prophet sent by *Allah* (Arabic for God). The word *Islam* means 'submission' and Muslims believe they must obey God totally and live by the holy book *The Koran*.

- **Hinduism** is almost 4,000 years old. Hindus worship many gods, but all believe in *dharma*, the right way to live. Like Buddhists, Hindus believe we all have past lives. By following the *dharma*, we may reach the perfect state of *Moksha* and so need never be born again.

- **Christianity** is split into three branches: Catholics whose leader is the Pope in Rome; Protestants; and the Eastern Orthodox church. Islam is split into Sunnis and Shi'ites. Shi'ites are the majority in Iraq and Iran.

- **Buddhism** is the religion of 300 million SE Asians. It is based on the teachings of Prince Siddhartha Gautama, the Buddha, who lived in NE India from 563 to 483BC.

- **Judaism** is the religion of Jews. They were the first to believe in a single god, who they called *Yahweh*, over 4,000 years ago. There are over 11 million Jews living outside Israel and 3.5 million living in Israel.

- **Most of the world's** major religions except for Hinduism are monotheistic – that is, they believe in just one God.

- **Three million Muslims** visit their holy city of Mecca in Saudi Arabia every year on pilgrimage.

- **Jains** of India will not take any form of life. They eat neither meat nor fish, nor, usually, eggs. Jain priests often sweep paths in front of them as they go to avoid stepping on insects.

> ★ STAR FACT ★
> The Hindu holy text, the *Mahabharata*, is the longest poem ever written, with around 200,000 verses.

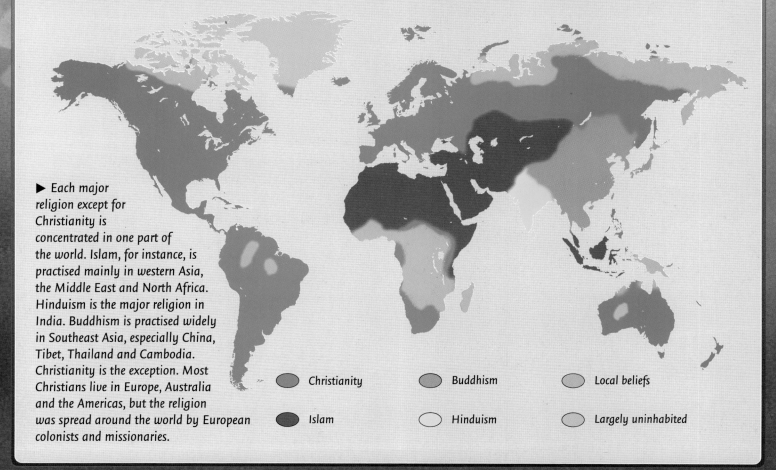

▶ Each major religion except for Christianity is concentrated in one part of the world. Islam, for instance, is practised mainly in western Asia, the Middle East and North Africa. Hinduism is the major religion in India. Buddhism is practised widely in Southeast Asia, especially China, Tibet, Thailand and Cambodia. Christianity is the exception. Most Christians live in Europe, Australia and the Americas, but the religion was spread around the world by European colonists and missionaries.

Christianity

Islam

Buddhism

Hinduism

Local beliefs

Largely uninhabited

# Peoples of the Middle East

- **People have farmed** in the Middle East longer than anywhere else in the world.

- **The Middle East** was the site of the first cities and ancient civilizations such as those of Sumer and Babylon.

- **Most people** in the Middle East are Arabs.

- **Arabic is spoken** in all Middle East countries except for Iran where Farsi (Persian) is spoken, Turkey where most speak Turkish and Israel where most speak Hebrew.

- **Most people** in the Middle East are Muslims, but Lebanon has many Christians and Israel is mostly Jewish.

- **Many of the Arab** countries of the Middle East – except Israel – are

▲ *Many people in the Middle East wear traditional Arab head coverings.*

dominated by Islamic traditions.

- **Islamic countries** of the Middle East are often ruled by kings and emirs, sultans and sheikhs who have absolute power. Yemen is a socialist republic; Turkey and Israel are republics. Iraq is a republic but it is ruled by President Saddam Hussein with absolute power.

- **The Jews of Israel** are locked in a conflict with the Arab people which dates back thousands of years.

- **The people of the United Arab Emirates** (UAE) are among the richest in the world, with a yearly income of almost $20,000 each.

- **The people of Yemen** are among the poorest in the world, with a yearly income of just $270 each.

# Central America

- **Central American countries** are: Mexico, Guatemala, Belize, Honduras, El Salvador, Nicaragua, Costa Rica and Panama.

- **Mexico:** Capital: Mexico City. Population: 94.3 million. Currency: Peso. Language: Spanish.

- **Mexico City** is the world's second largest city after Tokyo, with a population of 16.6 million.

▼ *The Panama Canal cuts right across Central America to link the Atlantic and Pacific Oceans and save ships huge journeys.*

- **Most Central American** countries were torn apart by revolution and civil war in the 1900s, but are now quiet.

- **Mexico owes** more money in foreign debt than any country but Brazil (almost $150 billion) and pays over $37 billion a year back to other countries.

- **Much land** is used for 'cash crops' (crops that can be sold abroad for cash) like coffee rather than for food.

- **Many Central Americans** work the land, growing food for themselves or labouring on plantations.

- **Maize** (corn) has been grown in Mexico for 7,000 years to make things such as tortillas (cornflour pancakes).

- **Bananas** are the most important export in Central American countries, forming a third of Honduras's entire exports. While bananas are grown on lowlands, coffee beans are important exports for highland regions, especially in Nicaragua, Guatemala, Costa Rica and El Salvador.

- **Most of Mexico's people** are mestizos, descendants of both Spanish settlers and American Indians.

# Georgia & neighbours

◄ Georgia, Armenia and Azerbaijan lie in a band between the Black Sea and the Caspian Sea. Georgia and Armenia are mountainous. Azerbaijan is quite flat.

● **Georgia:** Capital: Tbilisi. Population: 5.4 million. Currency: Lari. Language: Georgian.

● **Armenia:** Capital: Yerevan. Population: 3.8 million. Currency: Dram. Language: Armenian.

● **Azerbaijan:** Capital: Baku. Population: 7.7 million. Currency: Manat. Language: Azeri.

● **Georgia, Azerbaijan and Armenia** were once part of the Soviet Union.

● **In Georgia more people** live to be 100 years old than anywhere else in the world.

● **Georgia's capital Tbilisi** is said to be one of the world's oldest cities.

● **The oil** under the Caspian Sea off Azerbaijan once helped the Soviet Union produce half the world's oil. Villages on floating platforms house oilworkers.

● **New oil strikes** suggest there is 200 billion barrels of oil under the Caspian Sea – as much as Iran and Iraq combined.

● **Oil has made** some people around the Caspian Sea rich, while others have remained desperately poor.

● **America, Russia** and other countries are locked in dispute over the route for oil pipelines from the Caspian Sea.

# South Africa

◄ Nelson Mandela was the hero of the struggle against apartheid in South Africa. In 1994 he became the country's first president elected by all the people.

● **Capital:** Pretoria. Area: 1,225,815 sq km. Currency: Rand. Languages: 9 African languages including Zulu, plus English and Afrikaans.

● **Physical features:** Highest mountain: Champagne Castle (3,375 m). Longest river: the Orange (2,173 km).

● **Population:** 38.8 million. Population density: 31/sq km. Life expectancy: men 51.5 years; women 58.1 years.

● **Wealth:** GDP: $130.2 billion. GDP per head: $3,210.

> ★ STAR FACT ★
> In the 1900s, almost half the world's gold came from South Africa.

● **Exports:** Gold, diamonds, metals, metal products, machinery, citrus fruit, wine.

● **Until 1991** people of different races in South Africa were separated by law. This was called apartheid.

● **Apartheid** meant many black people were forced to live in specially built townships such as Soweto. Townships are far from cities and workplaces, so workers must commute for hours each day on crowded buses.

● **South Africa** has three capital cities. The administration is in Pretoria, the courts are in Bloemfontein and parliament is in Cape Town.

● **South Africa** produces more diamonds than all of the rest of the world put together.

# Germany

▲ Neuschwanstein, built for 'Mad' King Ludwig II of Bavaria in the 1870s, is the most famous of the many castles in Bavaria and Germany's Rhineland.

▶ The flatter northern part of Germany is a mixture of heath, marsh and rich farmland, where cereals such as rye are widely grown. The south is mountainous, with powerful rivers flowing through deep, wooded valleys.

Hamburg is Germany's biggest port

Germany's northwest is known as Saxony

When trees began to die from acid rain in the famous Black Forest, many Germans became committed to the Green cause. The country now has strong environment protection laws

Germany's longest river, the Rhine rises in the high Alpine mountains in the country's south

- **Capital:** Berlin. Area: 357,868 sq km. Currency: Deutschemark. Language: German.

- **Physical features:** Highest mountain: Zugspitze (2,963 m). Longest river: the Danube (2,859 km).

- **Population:** 82.1 million. Population density: 229/sq km. Life expectancy: men 73.9 years; women 80.2 years.

- **Wealth:** GDP: $2,321 billion. GDP per head: $28,280.

- **Exports:** Machinery, vehicles, chemicals, iron, steel, textiles, food, wine.

- **Germany** is the world's third biggest industrial nation after the USA and Japan, famous for its precision engineering and quality products, such as tools and machine tools.

- **Germany's smoky industrial** heartland was the Ruhr valley, where dozens of coal mines fed huge steelworks. Many mines and steelworks have now closed and many

people have moved south to places like Stuttgart and Munich to escape unemployment and dirty air. But the Ruhr remains important to industry.

- **Germany is** the world's third biggest car-maker after the USA and Japan. It is well known for its upmarket cars such as Mercedes, BMW and Audi.

- **German farms** are often small, family-run affairs. Yet the country can grow almost all its own food – growing huge quantities of cereal and sugar beet, and raising large numbers of cows and pigs.

> ★ STAR FACT ★
> The reunification of Germany in 1990 made it western Europe's biggest country by far.

# North Africa

- **Morocco:** Capital: Rabat. Population: 26.9 million. Currency: Dirham. Language: Arabic.

- **Algeria:** Capital: Algiers. Population: 29.4 million. Currency: Algerian dinar. Language: Arabic.

- **Tunisia:** Capital: Tunis. Population: 9.2 million. Currency: Tunisian dinar. Language: Arabic.

- **Libya:** Capital: Tripoli. Population: 5.2 million. Currency: Libyan dinar. Language: Arabic.

- **Much of** the world's phosphate supply comes from Morocco and Tunisia.

- **Algeria, Libya and Tunisia** all have large reserves of oil and gas.

- **People in Morocco,** Tunisia and Algeria eat a lot of

> ★ STAR FACT ★
> Libya is building the 600 km Great Manmade River, the world's longest water pipe, to supply towns in the desert.

couscous. Couscous is made from wheat which is pounded into hard grains of semolina, then steamed until soft. The couscous is then served with stewed lamb or vegetables.

- **The Moroccan** custom is to eat using the left hand rather than knives and forks.

- **The historic cities** of Fez and Marrakesh in Morocco are famous for their colourful souks or markets, where thousands of tourists each year come to haggle over beautiful hand-woven carpets, leather goods and jewellery.

▶ The countries of northwest Africa have warm, Mediterranean climates and farmers grow things like olives and citrus fruits.

# Pacific food

- **Most places** around the Pacific are near the sea, so fish plays an important part in diets.

- **In Japan** fish is often eaten raw in thin slices called sashimi, or cooked with vegetables in batter as a dish called tempura, often served with soy sauce.

- **At home** most Japanese eat traditional foods including rice and noodles, as well as fish, tofu and vegetables or eggs.

- **When out,** many Japanese people eat American-style foods from fast food restaurants.

▶ Lightly grilled or barbecued giant prawns and other seafood play a major role in Pacific food.

- **The Japanese** eat only half as much rice now as they did in 1960, as younger people prefer bread and doughnuts.

- **Younger Japanese** people have a diet richer in protein and fat than their parents', so grow 8-10 cm taller.

- **Pacific islanders** traditionally ate fish like bonito and tuna and native plants like breadfruit, coconuts, sweet potatoes and taro. They made flour from sago palm pith.

- **Many islanders** now eat nothing but canned Western food and suffer malnutrition.

- **Philippino** food is a mix of Chinese, Malay, American and Spanish. *Adobo* is chicken and pork in soy sauce.

- **Some Australians** now often eat 'fusion' food which blends Asian with European cooking styles.

# London

▲ London's Houses of Parliament and its tower with its bell Big Ben were built in 1860 after a fire destroyed an earlier building.

- **London** is the capital of the United Kingdom and its largest city by far, with a population of about 7 million.
- **People have settled** here for thousands of years, but the city of London began with the Roman city of Londinium.
- **Throughout the 19th century** London was the world's biggest city, with a million people, and the hub of the world's largest empire, the British Empire.

- **London** is based on two ancient cities: the City of London, which developed from the Roman and Saxon towns, and Westminster, which developed around the palaces of English kings around 1,000 years ago.
- **London** has 500,000 factory workers, but most people work in services, such as publishing and other media. London is one of the world's major finance centres.
- **Eight million tourists** come to London each year.
- **London's tallest building** is 244 m Canary Wharf tower.
- **The London Eye** is the biggest wheel in the world, giving people a bird's eye view over London.
- **London's oldest large buildings** are the Tower of London and Westminster Abbey, both 1,000 years old. The Tower of London was built for William the Conqueror.

★ STAR FACT ★
700,000 people work in banking and finance – more than in any other city in the world.

# Iraq and Iran

- **Iran:** Capital: Tehran. Population: 64.6 million. Currency: Iranian rial. Language: Persian (Farsi).
- **Iraq:** Capital: Baghdad. Population: 21.2 million. Currency: Iraqi dinar. Language: Arabic.
- **Iran is the largest** non-Arabic country in the Middle East. Iranians are descended from Persians.
- **Iran was once** called Persia, and was the centre of an empire ruled by the Shah that dates back thousands of years. The last Shah was overthrown in 1979.
- **Iran is an Islamic** country, and the strong views of religious leader Ayatollah Khomeini (who died in 1989) played a key role in the revolution in 1979, which brought him to power.

▶ Iraq and Iran are mostly hot, dry countries, but Iran is much more mountainous, ringed by the Zagros and Elburz mountains.

- **Iran is famous for its carpets,** often called Persian carpets. They are Iran's second largest export, after oil. Oil brings Iran 80% of its export earnings.
- **Iraq** was the place where civilization probably began 7,000 years ago. The Greeks called it Mesopotamia.
- **Since 1979** Iraq has been ruled by Saddam Hussein and his leadership has brought the country into conflict with much of the world – especially when he invaded Kuwait and started the Gulf War in 1991 when the USA and other nations retaliated.
- **Only about** a sixth of Iraq is suitable for farming and so it has to import much of its food, but it is one of the world's major oil producers.
- **United Nations** sanctions applied after the Gulf War still restrict trade with Iraq. Some argue that it is poor Iraqis who suffer from these and not Saddam Hussein.

# West Africa

- **West African countries** are: Mauritania, Mali, Burkina Faso, Senegal, Gambia, Guinea Bissau, Liberia, Guinea, Ivory Coast, Ghana, Sierra Leone, Togo, Benin and São Tomé and Prîncipe. All have populations under 10 million except for Ghana, Ivory Coast and Mali.

- **Ghana:** Capital: Accra. Population: 18.7 million. Currency: Cedi. Language: English.

- **Ivory Coast:** Capital: Yamoussoukro. Population: 13.6 million. Currency: CFA franc. Language: French.

- **Mali:** Capital: Bamako. Population: 10.4 million. Currency: CFA franc. Language: French.

- **West Africa** grows over half the world's cocoa beans.

- **Yams** are a vital part of the diet of people in West Africa, often providing breakfast, dinner and tea.

- **West Africa** is rich in gold and diamonds, which once sustained the ancient civilization of Mali and its famous capital of Timbuktu.

▲ *Ivory Coast alone grows a third of the world's cocoa beans. Here beans are drying in the sun.*

- **Ghana and Guinea** are rich in bauxite (aluminium ore).

- **Ghana** was called Gold Coast by Europeans because of the gold offered by the Ashanti peoples there.

- **Ghana** is still poor, but under President Gerry Rawlings, many of its young people are the best educated in Africa.

# Peoples of North America

- **80%** of the population of North America are white descendants of immigrants from Europe.

- **Among the smaller groups** 12% are black, 3% are Asian and 1% are American Indians.

- **Hispanics** are descended from a mix of white, black and American Indian people from Spanish-speaking countries of Latin America such as Mexico, Puerto Rico and Cuba. 9% of the US population is Hispanic.

- **92%** of the population of the USA was born there. Many new immigrants are Hispanic.

- **The original peoples** of North America were the American Indians who were living here for thousands of years before Europeans arrived.

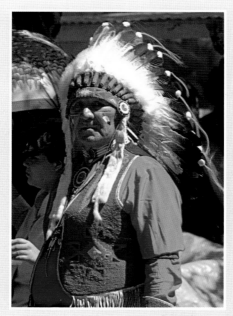

▲ *The original peoples of North America were the Indians, but they have been overwhelmed by European settlers.*

- **The native people** of America were called Indians by the explorer Christopher Columbus, but they have no collective name for themselves. Most American Indians prefer to be identified by tribe.

- **There are about** 540 tribes in the USA. The largest are the Cherokee, Chuppewa, Choctaw, Navajo and Sioux.

- **Most black Americans** are descendants of Africans brought here as slaves from 1600 to 1860.

- **Most European** immigrants were from Britain, so the main language is English.

- **Spanish** is spoken by many Americans and French is spoken by most Canadians.

# The Amazon

- **The Amazon River** in South America is the world's second longest river (6,439 km), and carries far more water than any other river.

- **The Amazon basin** – the area drained by the Amazon and its tributaries – covers over 7 million sq km and contains the world's largest tropical rainforest.

- **Temperatures** in the Amazon rainforest stay about 27°C all year round.

- **The Amazon rainforest** contains more species of plant and animal than anywhere else in the world.

- **The Amazon is home** to 30,000 different plants, 1,500 kinds of bird, and 3,000 species of fish in its rivers.

- **Manaus** in the Amazon basin has a population of over a million and a famous 19th century opera house.

> ★ **STAR FACT** ★
> The Amazon basin is home to 30 million different kinds of insect.

▲ In its upper reaches in the Andes, the Amazon tumbles over 5,000 m in the first 1,000 km.

- **Since the 1960s** the Brazilian government has been building highways and airports in the forest.

- **10%** of the forest has been lost for ever as trees are cut for wood, or to clear the way for gold-mining and ranching.

- **Forest** can sometimes regrow, but has far fewer species.

# Egypt and neighbours

- **Egypt:** Capital: Cairo. Population: 64.7 million. Currency: Egyptian pound. Language: Arabic.

- **Ethiopia:** Capital: Addis Ababa. Population: 58.2 million. Currency: Ethiopian birr. Language: Amharic.

- **Sudan:** Capital: Khartoum. Population: 27.7 million. Currency: Sudanese dinar. Language: Arabic.

- **Egypt relies** heavily on tourists visiting its ancient sites, like the 4,700 year-old Great Pyramid of Cheops at Giza.

- **99% of Egyptians** live by the River Nile which provides water for farming, industry and drinking. The world's largest reservoir, Lake Nasser, was created when the Nile was dammed by the Aswan High Dam.

- **Cairo** has a population of ten million and is growing so rapidly there are major housing and traffic problems.

- **Lots of cotton** is grown in Egypt and the Sudan.

- **Sudan is the largest** country in Africa.

- **In the 1980s and 1990s** the people of Ethiopia, Sudan and Somalia suffered dreadful famine. Many people here are still very poor and without enough to eat.

- **Grasslands south of the Sahara** are dotted with acacia thorn trees which ooze a liquid called gum arabic when their bark is cut. This was used in medicine and inks.

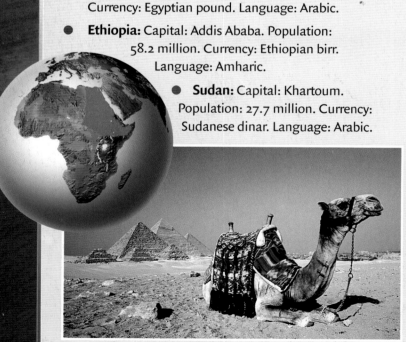

◄ Camels have provided desert transport in Egypt for thousands of years. The pyramids of the pharaohs are in the background.

# Australia

- **Capital:** Canberra. Area: 7,682,300 sq km. Currency: Australian dollar. Language: English.

- **Physical features:** Highest mountain: Mt Kosciusko (2,228 m). Longest river: the Darling (2,739 km).

- **Population:** 18.3 million. Population density: 2/sq km. Life expectancy: men 75.5 years; women 81.1 years.

- **Wealth:** GDP: $394 billion. GDP per head: $20,650.

- **Exports:** Ores and minerals, coal, oil, machinery, gold, diamonds, meat, wool, cereals.

- **Australia** is the only country that is also a continent.

- **Most of Australia** is so dry only 2% is good for growing crops, although the country sells a lot of wheat.

- But huge areas are used for rearing cattle and sheep, many raised on vast farms called 'stations'. Australia is also famous for its wines.

- **Australia has huge amounts** of iron, aluminium, zinc, gold and silver. The Mount Goldsworthy mine in Western Australia alone is thought to have 15 billion tonnes of iron ore. Broken Hill in New South Wales is the world's largest silver mine.

- **Australia's mild climate** encourages outdoor activities like surfing. Thousands head for Bondi Beach near Sydney on Christmas Day for a party or to surf. Australia is also the world's top cricketing nation.

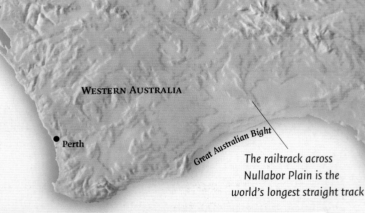

Darwin
Arnhem Land
Gulf of Carpentaria
Kimberley Plateau
Great Barrier Reef
Great Sandy Desert
QUEENSLAND
Alice Springs
Great Artesian Basin
Lake Eyre
Brisbane
WESTERN AUSTRALIA
Flinders Ranges
Perth
Great Australian Bight
Sydney
CANBERRA
The railtrack across Nullabor Plain is the world's longest straight track
Adelaide
Mt Kosciusko
Melbourne
The Great Dividing Range divides the moist coastal plain from the dry outback
Bass Strait
TASMANIA
Hobart

▲ Australia is the world's smallest continent but sixth biggest country. Much of it is dry and thinly populated. Most people live in the southeast or along the coast.

★ **STAR FACT** ★
Australia's 140 million sheep produce more than a third of the world's wool.

# Grand Canyon

- **The Grand Canyon** in Arizona in the southwest USA is one of the most spectacular gorges in the world.

- **The Grand Canyon** is about 450 km long and and varies in width from less than 1 km to over 30 km.

- **In places** the Grand Canyon is so narrow that motorcycle stunt riders have leaped right across from one side to the other.

- **The Grand Canyon** is about 1,600 m deep, with almost sheer cliff sides in some places.

- **Temperatures** in the bottom of the Canyon can be as much as 14°C hotter than they are at the top, and the bottom of the Canyon gets only 180 mm of rain per year compared to 660 mm at the top.

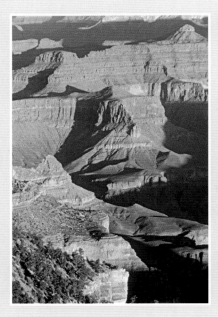

▲ *The shadows cast by the evening sun reveal the layer upon layer of rock in the steep sides of the Grand Canyon.*

- **The Grand Canyon** was cut by the Colorado River over millions of years as the whole Colorado Plateau was rising bit by bit. The bends in the river's course were shaped when it still flowed over the flat plateau on top, then the river kept its shape as it cut down through the rising plateau.

- **As the Colorado** cut down, it revealed layers of limestone, sandstone, shale and other rocks in the cliffs.

- **The Colorado** is one of the major US rivers, 2,334 km long.

- **The Hoover Dam** across the Colorado is one of the world's highest concrete dams, 221 m high.

- **The Hoover Dam** creates 185 km long Lake Mead, North America's biggest artificial lake.

# Peru and neighbours

- **Peru:** Capital: Lima. Area: 1,285,216 sq km. Currency: Nuevo Sol. Languages: Spanish and Quechua.

- **Physical features:** Highest mountain: Huascaran (6,768 m). Longest river: The Amazon (6,439 km).

- **Population:** 24.4 million. Population density: 18/sq km. Life expectancy: men 65.9 years; women 70.9 years.

- **Wealth:** GDP: $63.7 billion. GDP per head: $2,610.

- **Exports:** Copper, lead, fish products, iron, zinc, oil, coffee, llama and alpaca wool, cotton.

- **Peru** is the third largest country in South America. The coastal plain is desert, but Peru's biggest city Lima is here. Inland are the towering Andes mountains, where rivers have cut deep gorges.

- **Peru** was the home of the Inca Empire conquered by the Spaniard Francisco Pizarro in the 1520s. Now it has a larger Indian population than any other South American nation.

- **Peru** is a leading producer of copper, lead, silver and zinc, and a major fishing nation. But most people are poor, especially in the mountains. In the 1990s guerillas called *Sendero Luminoso* (Shining Path) and *Tupac Amaru* sparked off violent troubles.

- **Ecuador:** Capital: Quito. Population: 11.9 million. Currency: Sucre. Language: Spanish.

- **Bolivia:** Capital: La Paz. Population: 7.8 million. Currency: Sucre. Language: Spanish.

▶ *The llama was for centuries the main source of meat and wool and the main means of transport for people in Peru.*

# Kenya

- **Capital:** Nairobi. Area: 582,646 sq km. Currency: Kenyan shilling. Languages: Swahili and English.

- **Physical features:** Highest mountain: Mt Kenya (5,199 m). Longest river: Tana (800 km).

- **Population:** 33.8 million (est). Population density: 50/sq km. Life expectancy: men 51.1 years; women 53 years.

- **Wealth:** GDP: $9.7 billion. GDP per head: $340.

- **Exports:** Tea, coffee, fruit, flowers, vegetables, petroleum products.

- **Remains of early human ancestors** found by Lake Turkana show people have lived in Kenya for millions of years.

- **Much of Kenya** is a vast, dry, grassland plain, home to spectacular wildlife such as lions, giraffes and elephants. They attract thousands of tourists each year.

- **Most Kenyans** live on small farm settlements, raising crops and livestock for themselves, but there are big cash crop plantations for tea, coffee, vegetables and flowers.

- **Many Kenyans** are moving to the big cities: Nairobi and Mombasa.

- **Kenya's population** is growing rapidly – by 3% a year.

▼ Unlike most Kenyans, many Masai retain cattle herding as a way of life.

# Health and education

- **Progress** in medical science, better diet and improved hygiene have made the world a healthier place for many.

- **How long** people are likely to live is called life expectancy. In 1950, the world average was just 40 years. Now it is over 63 years.

- **Life expectancy** is usually high in richer countries. The Japanese live, on average for 80 years; the Swiss live for 78 years.

- **Life expectancy** is much lower in poor countries. People in Sierra Leone live just 37.2 years; people in Malawi live 39.3 years.

- **Vaccination programmes** have reduced the effects of some major diseases. The terrible disease smallpox was thought to be wiped out in 1977.

- **Some diseases** are on the increase in poorer parts of the world. AIDS (Acquired Immune Deficiency Syndrome) is now killing huge numbers of Africans.

- **In some parts** of the world, disease, lack of food and water and poor healthcare mean that one child in every four dies before reaching the age of five in poor countries like Afghanistan and Sierra Leone.

- **In the USA and Europe** less than one child in a hundred dies before the age of five.

- **In wealthier** countries such as the USA and Japan, there is on average one doctor for every 400 people.

- **In most poor African** countries, there is just one doctor for every 50,000 people.

▲ Death rates per thousand people vary from over 20 in many African countries to under 3 in many Arab countries of the Gulf.

# France

> ★ **STAR FACT** ★
> French vineyards produce more than a
> quarter of the world's wine every year.

- **Capital:** Paris. Area: 543,965 sq km. Currency: Franc.
  Language: French.

- **Physical features:** Highest mountain: Mont Blanc
  (4,807 m). Longest river: the Loire (1,005 km).

- **Population:** 58.5 million. Population density: 105/sq
  km. Life expectancy: men 74.2 years; women 82 years.

- **Wealth:** GDP: $1,542 billion. GDP per head: $26,300.

- **Exports:** Agricultural products, machinery,
  chemicals, food and wine.

- **France** is the biggest food producer in Europe,
  apart from Russia. In the north and west,
  wheat, sugar beet and many other crops
  are grown and dairy cattle are raised. In
  the warmer, drier south of France
  grapes and other
  fruit are grown.

▶ *France is famous
both for its beef
cattle, like this
Charolais, and its
dairy cows, which
give cheeses
including the
delicious soft cheeses
Brie and Camembert.*

- **France has limited** coal and oil reserves, but nuclear
  power gives France 75% of its energy.

- **France** is the biggest country in western Europe.
  Much is still rural, with ancient farmhouses and
  villages looking as if they have changed little in
  centuries. But French cities like Lyons and Marseilles
  are famous for their sophisticated culture. They are
  also the centres of so much industry that France
  is the world's fourth largest industrial
  nation after the USA, Japan and
  Germany.

- **The French**
  are traditionally
  famous for their
  *haute cuisine* (fine
  cooking) using
  the best
  ingredients, and
  creating fantastic
  table displays. Later,
  plainer styles
  developed and a lighter
  style of cooking called
  *nouvelle cuisine* (new
  cooking) has
  developed to suit
  today's tastes.

▶ *France
is a large and
enormously varied
country. In the
centre are the rugged
hills and volcanic peaks of
the Massif Central. To the
south is the warm sunny
Mediterranean coast. The
low, rolling countryside of
the north and west is
cooler. The highest
mountains are the Alps in
the southeast – rising to
Mont Blanc at
4,807 m– and the
Pyrenees in the
southwest, along the
border with Spain.*

Calais

Lille

English Channel

Le Havre

PARIS

CHAMPAGNE

Strasbourg

Vosges

BRITTANY

Le Mans

Tours

Avallon

Bay of Biscay

La Châtre

Jura

La Rochelle

Lyon

Mont Blanc ▲

Massif Central

Bordeaux

Bergerac

Alps

LANGUEDOC

PROVENCE

MONACO

Nice

Toulouse

Marseilles

Mediterranean Sea

Pyrenees

# Antarctica

- **Antarctica** is the fifth largest continent, larger than Europe and Australia, but 98% of it is under ice.

- **The Antarctic population** is made up mostly of scientists, pilots and other specialists there to do research in the unique polar environment.

- **About 3,000 people** live in Antarctica in the summer, but less than 500 stay all through the bitter winter.

- **The biggest community** in Antarctica is McMurdo which is home to up to 2,000 people in summer and has cafés, a cinema, a church and a nuclear power station.

- **People and supplies** reach McMurdo either on ice-breaker ships that smash through the sea ice, or by air.

- **McMurdo settlement** was built around the hut the British polar explorer Captain Scott put up on his 1902 expedition to the South Pole.

- **The Amundsen–Scott** base is located directly underneath the South Pole.

- **Antarctica** has a few valuable mineral resources including copper and chrome ores.

- **There is coal** beneath the Transarctic Mountains, and oil under the Ross Sea.

- **Under the Antarctic Treaty** of 1961, 12 countries agreed a ban on mining to keep the Antarctic unspoiled. They allow only scientific research.

◀ *Emperor penguins are among the few large creatures that can survive the bitter Antarctic winter. They breed on the ice cap itself.*

# Industry

▲ *Nearly every country in the world is becoming more and more industrialized. New industries include services like banking rather than traditional manufacturing.*

- **Primary industries** are based on collecting natural resources. They include farming, forestry, fishing, mining and quarrying.

- **Things made** by primary industries are called primary products or raw materials.

- **Primary industries** dominate the economies of poorer countries. Copper is 85% of Zambia's exports.

- **Primary products** are much less important in developed countries. Primary products earn just 2% of Japan's GDP.

- **Secondary industry** is taking raw materials and turning them into products from knives and forks to jumbo jets. This is manufacturing and processing.

- **Tertiary industries** are the service industries that provide a service, such as banking or tourism, not a product.

- **Tertiary industry** has grown enormously in the most developed countries, while manufacturing has shrunk.

- **'Postindustrialization'** means developing service industries in place of factories.

- **Tertiary industries** include internet businesses.

> ★ **STAR FACT** ★
> More than 70% of the UK's income now comes from tertiary industry.

# The Middle East

- **Saudi Arabia:** Capital: Riyadh. Population: 19.5 million. Currency: Riyal. Language: Arabic.

- **Yemen:** Capital: Sana. Population: 16.3 million. Currencies: Yemeni dinar, riyal. Language: Arabic.

- **Kuwait:** Capital: Kuwait City. Pop: 1.7 m. Curr: Kuwaiti dinar. Language: Arabic.

- **United Arab Emirates (UAE):** Capital: Abu Dhabi. Population: 2.3 million. Currency: Dirham. Language: Arabic.

- **Population:** Oman: 2.3 million. Bahrain: 600,000. Qatar: 600,000.

- **Much of the Middle East** is desert. Rub'al Khali in Saudi lives up to its name, Empty Quarter. Tent-dwelling nomads called Bedouins have herded sheep and goats here for thousands of years. Now most Bedouins live in houses.

- **Oil has made** the Arab states rich. People in the UAE, Bahrain and Kuwait have a higher income per head than any country outside Europe.

- **Saudi Arabia** is the world's leading exporter of oil and second only to Russia as oil producer. It has 25% of the world's known oil reserves.

- **Yemen** is one of the world's poorest countries.

- **The oil-rich states** along the Gulf are short of water. Most comes from wells, but now they are building desalination plants which remove salt so they can use water from the sea.

◀ Civilization began in the Middle East, but the climate dried and turned much of it to desert.

# The Russian steppes

- **The steppes** are a vast expanse of temperate grassland, stretching right across Asia.

- **'Steppes'** is the Russian word for grassland.

- **The Western Steppe** extends 4,000 km from the grassy plains of the Ukraine through Russia and Kazakhstan to the Altai mountains on the Mongolian border.

- **The steppes** extend 300-800 km from north to south.

**★ STAR FACT ★**
The steppes extend 8,000 km across Eurasia, a fifth of the way round the world.

- **The Eastern Steppe** extends 2,500 km from the Altai across Mongolia to Manchuria in north China.

- **The Eastern Steppe** is higher and colder than the Western Steppe and the difference between winter and summer is as extreme as anywhere on Earth.

- **Nomadic herders** have lived on the steppes for over 6,000 years.

- **It was on the steppes** near the Black and Caspian Seas that people probably first rode horses 5,000 years ago.

- **The openness** of the steppes meant that travel by horse was easy long before roads were built.

◀ The steppes have supported nomadic herding people for thousands of years, but their way of life is slowly dying out.

# American food

▲ *The American hamburger has been spread around the world by fast-food chains. The American people eat 45,000 hamburgers every minute!*

- **Many American** foods were brought from Europe by immigrants.

- **Hamburgers** were brought to the USA by German immigrants in the 1800s, but are now the most famous American food.

- **Frankfurters** came from Frankfurt in Germany. They were christened 'hot dogs' by journalist Thomas Dorgan when a stall selling them in a roll opened on New York's Coney Island in 1916.

- **The pizza** came from Naples in Italy, but the first pizzeria opened in New York in 1905. Pizzas caught on after 1945.

- **Legend says** the bagel began in Vienna in 1683 as a stirrup-shaped bun made in honour of John III of Poland's horseback defence of the city against the Turks. It was taken to New York by Jewish immigrants.

- **Self-service** cafeterias began in the 1849 San Francisco Gold Rush.

- **The world's first** fast-food restaurant may have been the White Castle which opened in Wichita, Kansas in 1921.

- **The world's biggest** fast-food chain is McDonalds which has nearly 20,000 branches worldwide.

- **Pies** have been popular in the US since colonial times, and apple pie is the symbol of American home cooking.

- **American home cooking** includes beef steaks, chicken and ham with potatoes plus a salad. But Americans eat out often – not only fast-food such as hamburgers and French fries, but Chinese, Italian and Mexican dishes.

# Southern Africa

- **Mozambique:** Capital: Maputo. Population: 18.4 million. Currency: Metical. Language: Portuguese.

- **Angola:** Capital: Luanda. Population: 11.7 million. Currency: Kwanza. Language: Portuguese.

- **Zambia:** Capital: Lusaka. Pop: 8.6 million. Currency: Kwacha. Language: English.

- **Population:** Namibia: 1.6 million. Botswana: 1.5 million. Swaziland: 900,000.

- **Large areas** of southern African countries are too dry to farm intensively. Most people grow crops such as maize or raise cattle to feed themselves.

- **In Mozambique** plantations grow crops like tea and coffee for export, but most people who work on them are poor.

- **In 2000** much of Mozambique was devastated by huge floods from the Zambezi and Limpopo Rivers.

- **Zambia is the** world's fourth largest copper producer and relies on copper for 85% of its export earnings.

- **Namibia is the** world's second largest lead producer.

- **Namibia** has the world's biggest uranium mine and an estimated three billion carats of diamond deposits.

▼ *The vast Namib and Kalahari deserts cover much of Namibia and Botswana with sand and dust. Even beyond the deserts, vegetation is sparse and the living poor – except in the mines.*

# Tokyo

- **Tokyo** is the world's biggest city. With the port of Yokohama and the cities of Chiba and Kawasaki, it makes an urban area that is home to almost 30 million people.
- **Tokyo** is Japan's capital and leading industrial and financial centre.
- **Tokyo's stock exchange** is one of the world's three giants, along with London and New York.
- **Tokyo** was originally called Edo when it first developed as a military centre for the Shoguns. It was named Tokyo in 1868 when it became imperial capital.
- **14,000 people** live in every square kilometre of Tokyo – twice as many as in the same area in New York.
- **Some hotels** in Tokyo have stacks of sleeping cubicles little bigger than a large refrigerator.

▲ *Tokyo is perhaps the busiest, most crowded city in the world.*

> ★ STAR FACT ★
> Tokyo probably has more neon signs than any other city in the world.

- **During rush hours** *osiyas* (pushers) cram people on to commuter trains crowded with 10 million travellers a day.
- **Traffic police** wear breathing apparatus to cope with traffic fumes.
- **Tokyo mixes** the latest western-style technology and culture with traditional Japanese ways.

# Canada

- **Capital:** Ottawa. Area: 9,970,610 sq km. Currency: Canadian dollar. Languages: French and English.
- **Physical features:** Highest mountain: Mt Logan (5,951 m). Longest river: the Mackenzie, linked to the Peace by the Great Slave Lake (4,241 km).
- **Population:** 30.3 million. Population density: 3/sq km. Life expectancy: men 76.1 years; women 81.8 years.

- **Wealth:** GDP: $608 billion. GDP per head: $19,640.
- **Exports:** Vehicles and parts, machinery, petroleum, aluminium, timber, wood pulp, wheat.
  - **Canada** is the world's second largest country.
  - **Three-quarters** of Canada's small population live within 100 km of the southern border with the USA; the rest of the country is rugged and only thinly inhabited.
  - **Only 7%** of Canada is farmed, but this is a big area. The Prairie provinces – Saskatchewan, Alberta and Manitoba – grow a lot of wheat and raise many cattle.
  - **Canada** has 10% of the world's forest and is the world's largest exporter of wood products and paper.
- **The Inuit people** of the far north in the Arctic were given their own homeland of Nunavut in 1999.

◀ *The completion of the Canadian Pacific railroad right across Canada in 1885 was one of the great engineering feats of the 1800s.*

# Energy

- **Humans** now use well over 100 times as much energy as they did 200 years ago, and the amount is rising.

- **Europe, North America and Japan** use 70% of the world's energy with just a quarter of the people.

- **Fossil fuels** are coal, oil and natural gas – fuels made from organic remains buried and fossilized over millions of years. Fossil fuels provide 90% of the world's energy.

- **Fossil fuel** pollutes the atmosphere as it burns, causing health problems, acid rain and also global warming.

- **Fossil fuel** is non-renewable. This means it can't be used again once burned. At today's rates, the world's coal and oil will be burned in 60 years and its natural gas in 220 years.

- **Renewable energy** like running water, waves, wind and sunlight will not run out. Nuclear energy is non-renewable, but uses far less fuel than fossil fuel.

- **Alternative energy** is energy from sources other than fossil fuels and nuclear power. It should be renewable and clean.

- **Major alternative energy** sources are waves, geothermal, tides, wind and hydro-electric power.

Food for living

Home

Industry

Transport

Energy use in developed countries

Energy use in less developed countries

◀▼ Each person in developed countries uses 10 times as much energy as each person in less developed countries.

- **The Sun** provides the Earth with about the same as 500 trillion barrels of oil in energy a year – 1,000 times as much as the world's oil reserves. Yet little is used. Solar panels provide just 0.01% of human energy needs.

▼ *The pie diagram in the centre shows how much of the world's energy is provided by different sources. The top layer shows proportions ten years ago. The bottom layer shows proportions now. See how biomass energy use has risen.*

> ★ **STAR FACT** ★
> The average American uses 340 times as much energy as the average Ethiopian.

*Oil is our most important energy source, now providing almost 40% of the world's energy needs. The biggest reserves are around the Caspian Sea and in the Middle East.*

*Coal still provides almost 30% of the world's energy needs. Two-thirds of the world's reserves are in China, Russia and the USA. India and Australia are major producers too.*

*Wood and dried animal dung – called biomass – provide the main fuel for half the world's population. In some poorer countries, it provides 90% of all fuel.*

*Natural gas provides over 20% of world energy needs, and the proportion is rising. The biggest reserves are in Russia, the USA and Canada.*

*Hydrolectric power (HEP) uses fast-flowing rivers or water flowing through a dam to generate electricity. HEP supplies 7% of world energy needs.*

*Nuclear power now provides about 5% of the world's energy needs. The major producers are France, the USA and Russia.*

*Geothermal power uses heat from deep inside the Earth – either to heat water or make steam to generate electricity. Experts think geothermal use will go up.*

*Windpower, wavepower and solar energy produce barely 5% of the world's energy needs. The proportion is going up, but only very, very slowly.*

# Peoples of southern Asia

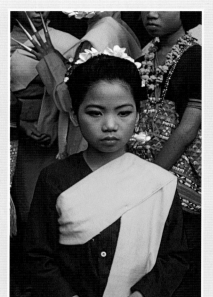

▶ Thai people are descended from peoples who migrated from southern China between AD200 and 1100.

- **There is a huge** variety of people living in southern Asia from India to the Philippines.

- **India** has hundreds of different ethnic groups speaking 30 languages and 1,500 dialects.

- **Indonesia** also has many different ethnic groups and over 250 different languages.

- **In Cambodia,** Vietnam, Thailand, Burma and Sri Lanka, people are mostly Buddhists.

- **In Indonesia**, Malaysia, Pakistan and Bangladesh, people are mostly Muslim.

- **In India,** 83% of people are Hindus.

- **The word Hindu** comes from the Indus river where Dravidian people created one of the world's great ancient civilizations 4,500 years ago.

- **By Hindu tradition** people are born into social classes called castes. Members of each caste can only do certain jobs, wear certain clothes and eat certain food.

- **Most Indians** are descended from both the Dravidians and from the Aryans who invaded and pushed the Dravidians into the south about 3,500 years ago.

- **The people of East Timor** in Indonesia are mainly Christian. Before they became independent they were under the oppressive rule of the Indonesian military government.

# Afghanistan & neighbours

- **Afghanistan:** Capital: Kabul. Population: 20.5 million. Currency: Afghani. Language: Pashto, Dari.

- **Tajikistan:** Capital: Dushanbe. Population: 5.5 million. Currency: Rouble. Language: Tajik.

- **Kyrgyzstan:** Capital: Bishkek. Population: 4.2 million. Currency: Som. Language: Kyrgyz.

- **Nepal:** Capital: Kathmandu. Population: 21.1 million. Currency: Nepalese rupee. Language: Nepali.

- **Tibet:** Capital: Lhasa. Population: 24.1 million. Tibet is not an independent state, but part of China.

- **These five countries** contain most of the world's highest mountains, including Everest (8,846 m) and Kanchenjunga (8,598 m) in Nepal and Garmo in Tajikistan (7,495 m).

- **The brilliant blue** gemstone lapis lazuli has been mined at Sar-e-Sang in Afghanistan for over 6,000 years.

- **Kyrgyzstan** has been independent from the USSR since 1991, but many people are Russian or half-Russian. Only a few still live in the traditional kyrgyz tents or 'yurts'.

- **Tajikistan** is still mostly rural, unlike Kyrgyzstan, and farmers in the deep valleys grow cotton and melons.

- **Afghanistan** was wracked by civil war until the fiercely Muslim Taliban came to power in the late 1990s and forced on the people a very harsh regime.

▼ These five countries are perched on top of the world's highest mountains, the Himalayas.

# Hungary and neighbours

▲ *Hungary is one of the world's leading producers of sunflower oil, and in summer vast areas of its Great Plain turn yellow with sunflower blooms.*

- **Hungary:** Capital: Budapest. Population: 10.3 million. Currency: Forint. Language: Hungarian.

- **Czech Republic:** Capital: Prague. Population: 10.3 million. Currency: Koruna. Language: Czech.

- **Slovakia:** Capital: Bratislava. Population: 5.4 million. Currency: Koruna. Language: Slovak.

- **Slovenia:** Capital: Ljubljana. Population: 1.9 million. Currency: Tolar. Language: Slovenian.

- **Until 1990** all of these countries were under Soviet rule, but they are all now democratic republics.

  - **Since 1990**, the historic city of Prague has become a popular destination, especially with the young, and many recording artists have worked in studios here.

  - **The Czech Republic** is famous for Pilsener beer brewed in the town of Pilsen with hops grown locally.

  - **Hungary's** national dish is *goulash*. This is a rich stew made from meat, onion and potatoes, spiced with paprika (red pepper) and served with black rye bread.

- **Slovakian people** were largely rural until recently, with a strong tradition of folk music, dancing and dress. Now many people are moving into industrial towns.

- **Vienna's white** Lippizaner horses are bred in Slovenia.

# Hong Kong

> **! NEWS FLASH !**
> The proposed Landmark tower in Kowloon could be 574 m tall.

- **Hong Kong** is a special city region on the south coast of China. It consists of a peninsula and 235 islands.

- **Hong Kong** was administered by the British from 1842 until July 1 1997.

- **Over six million** people are crowded into Hong Kong, mostly in the cities of Kowloon and Hong Kong itself.

- **Hong Kong** is one of the world's most bustling, dynamic, overcrowded cities. It makes huge amounts of textiles, clothing and other goods and is also one of the world's major financial and trading centres.

- **All but 2%** of Hong Kong people are Chinese, but many speak English as well as Chinese.

- **Hong Kong** is one of the world's three biggest ports, along with Rotterdam and Singapore.

- **Hong Kong** is the world's biggest container port.

- **Hong Kong's Chep Lap Kok** airport, opened in 1998, is one of the world's most modern airports.

- **The Hong Kong-Shanghai Bank** tower is one of the world's most spectacular modern office blocks.

▼ *Hong Kong is quite mountainous, so people are crowded on to a small area of land, often in huge, high-rise apartment blocks.*

# China

- **Capital:** Beijing. Area: 9,560,900 sq km. Currency: Yuan. Language: Mandarin.

- **Physical features:** Highest mountain: Qomolanjma (Mt Everest, 8,848 m). Longest river: Chang (Yangtse) (6,300 km).

- **Population:** 1,244.2 million. Population density: 127/sq km. Life expectancy: men 67.9 years; women 72 years.

- **Wealth:** GDP: $902 billion. GDP per head: $860.

- **Exports:** Machinery, textiles, clothing, crude oil, coal, tobacco, grains, canned food, fish products, raw silk.

- **China** is the world's third largest country, stretching from the soaring Himalayas in the west to the great plains of the Huang (Yellow) and Chang (Yangtse) rivers in the east where most people live.

- **China** is the most highly populated country in the world. In 1979, it was growing so rapidly the government made it illegal for couples to have more than one child. In the countryside, people disliked the law because extra children were needed to work the fields. In towns, the law worked better, but single children were often spoiled and so called 'Little Emperors'.

- **70%** of China's people still live and work on the land, growing rice and other crops to feed themselves. But as China opens up to western trade, so industry is growing in cities like Guangzhou (Canton) and more and more country people are going to work there.

- **China** became communist in 1949, and the nationalist government fled to the island of Taiwan. China and Taiwan still disagree over who should govern China. Taiwan now has its own thriving economy and makes more computer parts – especially microchips – than any other country in the world.

▲ Rice is grown all over China in flooded fields called paddies.

▲ With over 1,200 million inhabitants, China has more people than any other country. One in five people alive today are Chinese. China is also one of the world's oldest civilizations and Chinese cities date back at least 3,500 years. People were farming here long before the pharaohs came to power in Egypt.

The island province and city of Hong Kong was ruled by the British from 1842 onwards. It was returned to Chinese rule in 1997

# Netherlands and Belgium

- **Netherlands:** Capital: Amsterdam. Population: 15.6 million. Currency: Guilder. Language: Dutch.

- **Belgium:** Capital: Brussels. Population: 10.1 million. Currency: Belgian franc. Languages: Dutch, French and German.

- **Belgium and the Netherlands** are often called the Low Countries because they are both quite flat. The Netherlands' highest hill is just 321 m.

- **A third of the Netherlands** (also known as Holland) is polders – land once covered by the sea, but now protected by banks called dykes and pumped dry.

- **The Netherlands** exports more cheese than any other country in the world. Edam and Gouda are famous.

- **The Netherlands** is famous for its vast fields of tulips.

> ★ STAR FACT ★
> The Netherlands is the world's biggest trader in cut flowers.

- **Rotterdam** at the mouth of the Rhine is one of the world's biggest ports, handling a million tonnes of goods each day.

- **Brussels** is the seat of the European Union Commission and Council.

- **The Belgian** city of Antwerp is the diamond-cutting centre of the world.

▶ Holland is famous for its windmills. These are not for grinding flour but for working the pumps that keep the flat land dry.

# Peoples of South America

- **South America** has a population of a little over 500 million people.

- **Before its conquest** by the Spanish and Portuguese in the 16th century, South America was home to many native peoples.

- **There are native villages** in the Andes with only one race, and a few native tribes in the Amazon rainforest who have had little contact with the outside world.

- **The main population groups now** are American Indians, whites, blacks (whose ancestors were brought as slaves) and people of mixed race.

▶ In the Amazon, small tribes like the Matses still survive as they have done for thousands of years.

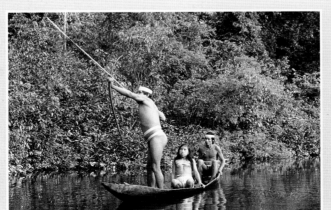

- **Most people** in Latin America are mixed race.

- **The largest mixed race** groups are mestizos (people with both American Indian and white ancestors) and mulattoes (people with black and white ancestors).

- **Mestizos** are the majority in countries such as Paraguay and Venezuela. Mulattoes are the majority in Brazil.

- **The Europeans** who came to South America were mostly Spanish and Portuguese, so nearly two-thirds of South Americans speak Spanish.

- **Many American Indians** speak their own languages.

- **Quechua** is a native language, which Peru has made its official language along with Spanish.

# Midwest USA

- **Huge amounts** of wheat and maize are grown on the damper eastern side of the vast rolling plains.

- **Millions** of beef cattle are raised on ranches in the drier west.

- **The weather is often extreme** here with scorching summer days and winter blizzards.

- **Tornado Alley** is a band through Kansas and beyond which is blasted by hundreds of tornadoes every summer.

- **Heavy farming** in the 1930s let dry winds strip away soil leaving just dust over a vast area called the Dust Bowl. Irrigation and windbreaks have lessened the problem.

- **Millions of buffalo (bison)** roamed the Great Plains 200 years ago. Now just 50,000 live on reserves.

◀ *The midwest is North America's agricultural heartland, raising millions of cattle and growing vast areas of yellow corn.*

- **Detroit** on the Great Lakes is the centre of the US car and truck industry. Ford, Chrysler and General Motors all have their headquarters here.

- **Detroit** is sometimes known as Motown (short for 'motor town') and was famous in the 1960s for its black soul 'Motown' music.

- **Many Italians** have emigrated to the USA and most US cities have an Italian area. Chicago's Italians invented their own deep, soft version of the pizza.

- **Chicago,** known as 'The Windy City', is the USA's third largest city, home to over three million people.

# Ireland

- **Capital (Eire):** Dublin. Area: 70,282 sq km. Currency: Punt. Languages: Irish and English. Over two-thirds of Ireland is in Eire, the Irish Republic. The rest is Northern Ireland or Ulster, which is part of the UK.

- **Physical features:** Highest mountain: Carrauntoohil (1,041 m). Longest river: the Shannon (386 km).

- **Population (Eire):** 3.6 million. Population density: 51/sq km. Life expectancy: men 73.6 years; women 79.2 years.

- **Wealth (Eire):** GDP: $65.1 billion. GDP per head: $17,790.

- **Exports:** Livestock, dairy

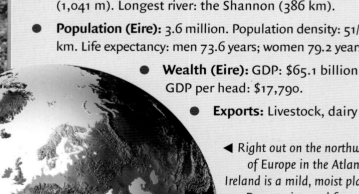

◀ *Right out on the northwest of Europe in the Atlantic, Ireland is a mild, moist place. Damp mists and frequent showers keep grass lush and green, earning the island the name 'The Emerald Isle'.*

products, whiskey, machinery, chemicals, electronics.

- **Peat** is one of Ireland's few natural energy resources. Peat is the compressed rotten remains of plants found in peat bogs. Once dried it can be burned as fuel.

- **Ireland** is still largely a poor farming country, famous for its pubs and folk music. But many young people are moving to the towns, or to other countries in search of work and a better lifestyle.

- **Ireland,** and Dublin in particular, have begun to thrive in recent years – partly because of the success of high-tech electronics and computer industries.

- **Entertainment** is big business in Ireland. Many films – both American and Irish – are made in Ireland, and pop, rock and folk music are huge money earners.

> ★ **STAR FACT** ★
> Ireland breeds more winning racehorses than any comparable country in Europe.

# North and South Korea

- **North Korea:** Capital: Pyongyang. Population: 23 million. Currency: Won. Language: Korean.

- **South Korea:** Capital: Seoul. Population: 45.7 million. Currency: Won. Language: Korean.

- **Korea** split into the communist North and capitalist South in 1948.

- **A bitter war** between North and South involving the USA ended with a treaty in 1953.

- **North and South Korea** both still have large armies. South Korea's has over half a million soldiers.

- **After the war** money from US banks helped the South become the world's fastest growing economy.

- **Huge factories** run by companies called chaebol churned out everything from computers to Hyundai and Daewoo cars.

- **South Korean shipyards** build one in six of the world's ships. Only Japan builds more.

- **In 1997** North Korea suffered food shortages after two years of floods followed by drought.

- **In 1997-98** the uncovering of massive government dishonesty made many South Korean businesses bankrupt. New President Kim Dae Jung has led a recovery.

◄ *The Korean company of Daewoo not only makes cars, but ships, computers, TVs, videos and much more besides.*

# Central Africa

- **Equatorial Guinea:** Capital: Malabo. Population: 400,000. Currency: CFA Franc. Language: Spanish.

- **Gabon:** Capital: Libreville. Population: 1.1 million. Currency: CFA franc. Language: French.

- **Congo (Brazzaville):** Capital: Brazzaville. Pop: 2.6 million. Currency: CFA franc. Language: French.

- **Cameroon:** Capital: Yaoundé. Population: 12.8 million. Currency: CFA Franc. Language: French and English.

- **Central African Republic (CAR):** Capital: Bangui. Population: 3.4 million. Currency: CFA Franc. Language: French.

- **French and English** are official languages, but most people speak their own African language.

- **Most Gabonese** are farmers, but Gabon is rich in iron and manganese and famous for its ebony and mahogany wood.

- **75% of people** in Cameroon are farmers, growing crops such as cassava, corn, millet, yams and sweet potatoes. Most of Cameroon's roads are dust roads.

- **Congo (Brazzaville)** is so called to distinguish it from neighbouring Congo (Kinshasa). It is the world's second poorest country. It is thickly forested and many people travel by dugout canoes. Many raise bananas or grow crops to feed themselves.

- **The CAR and Equatorial Guinea** are perhaps the least developed countries in Africa.

▶ *Cameroon, Gabon, CAR, Congo and Equatorial Guinea lie near the Equator, and are often thickly wooded with rainforest.*

# Nigeria and neighbours

- **Nigeria:** Capital: Abuja. Population: 103.9 million. Currency: Naira. Language: English.

- **Niger:** Capital: Niamey. Population: 9.8 million. Currency: CFA franc. Language: French.

- **Chad:** Capital: N'Djamena. Population: 7.1 million. Currency: CFA franc. Languages: Arabic and French.

- **Most people** in the north of Nigeria, and in Niger and Chad live by growing food for themselves.

- **The amount of rainfall** increases dramatically from north to south, and the vegetation changes from rainforest to dry grassland to desert in marked bands.

- **In the dry north** people grow mainly millet; in the moist south, they grow rice and roots such as cassava and yam, which they eat boiled with goat, chicken and fish.

- **Oil makes up 98%** of Nigeria's exports.

- **The money from oil** has made Nigeria among the most heavily urbanized and populous countries in Africa, especially around its main city Lagos.

- **Nigeria** is home to over 250 different peoples.

- **Nigeria** became a democracy again in 1998 after years of bitter civil war and military dictatorship, but tensions remain.

▼ *The position of Nigeria, Niger and Chad on the southern fringes of the Sahara desert makes them prone to drought as climate change and overgrazing push the desert further south.*

# Argentina

▼ *'Gaucho' means outcast, but the tough gauchos are Argentina's heroes.*

- **Capital:** Buenos Aires. Area: 2,766,889 sq km. Currency: Peso. Language: Spanish.

- **Physical Features:** Highest mountain: Aconcagua (6,960 m). Longest river: Paraná (3,943 km).

- **Population:** 35.6 million. Population density: 13/sq km. Life expectancy: men 69.7 years; women 76.8 years.

- **Wealth:** GDP: $325 billion. GDP per head: $8,950.

- **Exports:** Minerals, wheat, maize, meat, hides, wool, tannin, linseed oil, peanuts, processed foods.

- **The Argentinian landscape** is dominated by the pampas, the vast flat grasslands which stretch all the way to the high Andes mountains in the west.

- **Most of Argentina's** exports are pampas products – wheat, corn, meat, hides and wool.

- **Cattle** on the pampas – 50 million of them – are herded by Argentina's famous cowboys, the gauchos.

- **Argentina** is the most educated country in South America, with a third of students going to university.

> ★ **STAR FACT** ★
> Buenos Aires, with 12 million people, is the biggest city in the Southern Hemisphere.

# The United Kingdom

- **Capital:** London. Area: 242,534 sq km. Currency: Pound. Language: English.

- **Physical features:** Highest mountain: Ben Nevis (1,343 m). Longest river: the Severn (320 km).

- **Population:** 58.5 million. Population density: 239/sq km. Life expectancy: men 74.5 years; women 79.8 years.

- **Wealth:** GDP: $1,231 billion. GDP per head: $20,870.

- **Exports:** Manufactured goods such as chemicals and electronics, meat and dairy products, whisky, financial services, music and publishing.

- **The British Isles** are 4,000 islands with 20,000 km of coast. There are two large islands: Great Britain and Ireland. The United Kingdom (UK) is four countries joined politically – England, Scotland, Wales and N. Ireland.

- **England** is intensively farmed, especially in the south where wheat, barley, rape, sugar beet and vegetables are grown. In the moister west and north of England, especially, and Scotland and Wales, cattle and sheep are reared. The Welsh borders are famous for their orchards.

- **The Industrial Revolution** began in the UK. In the 1800s, heavy industries such as steelmaking and engineering grew in northern coalfield cities like Manchester and Leeds. Now coal's importance as an energy source has dwindled, and some smaller northern towns are finding it difficult to survive. But southern England is thriving on light industries and services.

- **London** is one of the world's great financial centres. Over 500 international banks are crammed into a small area of the city called the Square Mile. Here billions of dollars' worth of money deals are done every day.

▲ The Millennium Dome was erected by the River Thames in east London to celebrate the year 2000.

◄ England is the biggest and most densely populated of the countries of the UK – a lush land of rolling hills, rich farmland and big cities. Wales is a land of hills and sheep farms, except for the south where industry is important and coal was once mined in huge amounts. Much of Scotland is wild moors and valleys, and most people live in the central lowlands around the cities of Glasgow and Edinburgh. A third of Northern Ireland's population lives in Belfast.

**SCOTLAND**

Ben Nevis ▲

Grampian Mountains

Atlantic Ocean

EDINBURGH
Glasgow

Southern Uplands

**N. IRELAND**

BELFAST

North Sea

Irish Sea

**IRELAND**

DUBLIN

Manchester

Liverpool

Cambrian Mts.

St. George's Channel

Cork

**WALES**

Birmingham

**ENGLAND**

CARDIFF

Bristol

LONDON

Dover

English Channel

Plymouth

★ **STAR FACT** ★
Over 60% of the UK's workforce now work in financial and service industries.

# The Near East

- **Syria:** Capital: Damascus. Population: 14.9 million. Currency: Syrian pound. Language: Arabic.

- **Jordan:** Capital: Amman. Population: 6.1 million. Currency: Jordan dinar. Language: Arabic.

- **The Lebanon:** Capital: Beirut. Population: 3.1 million. Currency: Lebanese pound. Language: Arabic.

- **Damascus** was a major trading centre 4,000 years ago.

- **Syria** is at the western end of the belt of rich farmland known as the fertile crescent, which was the cradle of the earliest civilizations, along the banks of the Tigris and Euphrates rivers.

- **Most Syrian farmers** still work on small plots growing cotton and wheat. But 40% of Syrians now work in services.

- **Around 70% of Jordan's** income is from services like tourism and banking.

- **The people of Syria,** Jordan and Lebanon are mostly Arabs. 90% of Syrians and Jordanians are Muslims, but 40% of Lebanese are Christians.

- **In 1948** Palestine was split between Israel, Jordan and Egypt. Palestinian Arabs' desire for their own country has caused conflict with Israelis.

- **In 1996** Israeli troops withdrew from the Gaza strip region, and Palestinians elected their own local administration.

# Indian food

- **Most Indians** live on very plain diets – based on staples such as rice in the east and south, *chapatis* (flat wheat bread) in the north and northwest, and *bajra* (millet bread) in the Maharashtra region.

- **The staple foods** are supplemented by *dal* (lentil porridge), vegetables and yoghurt.

- **Chillis and other spices** such as coriander, cumin, ginger and turmeric add flavour.

- **Chicken and mutton** are costly and eaten occasionally. Hindus will not eat beef and Muslims will not eat pork.

- **Most Indian meals** are cooked in *ghee* (liquid butter). Ghee is made by heating butter to boil off water, then allowing it to cool and separate. Ghee is scooped off the top.

- **Although many Indians** have simple diets, India has an ancient and varied tradition of fine cooking.

- **Curries are** dishes made with a sauce including the basic Indian spices – turmeric, cumin, coriander and red pepper. The word curry comes from the Tamil *kari*, or sauce.

- **The basis of a curry** is a *masala*, a mix of spices, often blended with water or vinegar to make a paste.

- **Southern Indian** vegetable curries are seasoned with hot blends like *sambar podi*.

- **Classic northern Indian** Mughal dishes are often lamb, or chicken based, and seasoned with milder *garam masala*.

◀ *An Indian meal is rarely served on a single plate. Instead, it comes in different dishes, which diners dip into.*

# Paris

▲ *Les Halles was the main market for Paris from the 12th century, but in the 1970s was transformed into a sleek modern shopping centre.*

- **Paris** is the capital of France and its largest city with a population of just over two million.
- **Paris** is France's main business and financial centre. The Paris region is also a major manufacturing region, notably for cars.

- **Paris** is famed for luxuries like perfume and fashion.
- **Paris** is known for restaurants like La Marée, cafés like Deux Magots and nightclubs like the Moulin Rouge.
- **Paris** monuments include the Arc de Triomphe, the Eiffel Tower, Notre Dame cathedral and the Beauborg Centre.
- **Paris** gets its name from a Celtic tribe called the Parisii who lived there 2,000 years ago.
- **The Roman general** Julius Caesar said the Parisii were 'clever, inventive and given to quarrelling among themselves'. Some say this is true of Parisians today.
- **Paris** was redeveloped in the 1850s and 60s by Baron Haussman on the orders of Emperor Napoleon III.
- **Haussman** gave Paris broad, tree-lined streets called boulevards, and grand, grey, seven-storey houses.

> ★ **STAR FACT** ★
> Well over half of France's business deals are done in Paris.

# Balkan peninsula

- **The Balkan peninsula** is a mountainous region in SE Europe between the Adriatic and Aegean Seas.
- **The Balkans** include many different nations, which were under either the Austro-Hungarian or Turkish Empires until 1918.
- **From 1918 to 1991** Serbia, Croatia, Bosnia and Herzegovina, Macedonia, Slovenia, Montenegro and Kosovo were joined as communist Yugoslavia.
- **Bosnia** Herzegovina, Croatia, Macedonia, Slovenia and Kosovo broke away from Yugoslavia in the 1990s amid much bitter conflict.
- **Serbia** and Montenegro formed a smaller Yugoslavia in 1992 under Serbian President Milosevic. Many nations do not recognize this union.
- **Yugoslavia**: Capital: Belgrade. Population: 10.6 million. Currency: Dinar. Language: Serbo-croatian.
- **Croatia**: Capital: Zagreb. Population: 4.8 million. Currency: Kuna. Language: Serbo-croatian.

- **Bosnia**: Capital: Sarajevo. Population: 3.5 million. Currency: Bosnian dinar. Language: Serbo-croatian.
- **Albania**: Capital: Tirana. Population: 3.4 million. Currency: New lek. Language: Albanian.
- **Macedonia**: Capital: Skopje. Pop: 2.3 m. Curr: Denar. Language: Macedonian.

▼ *This ancient bridge at Mostar in Bosnia was a famous casualty of the wars of the 1990s.*

# Agriculture

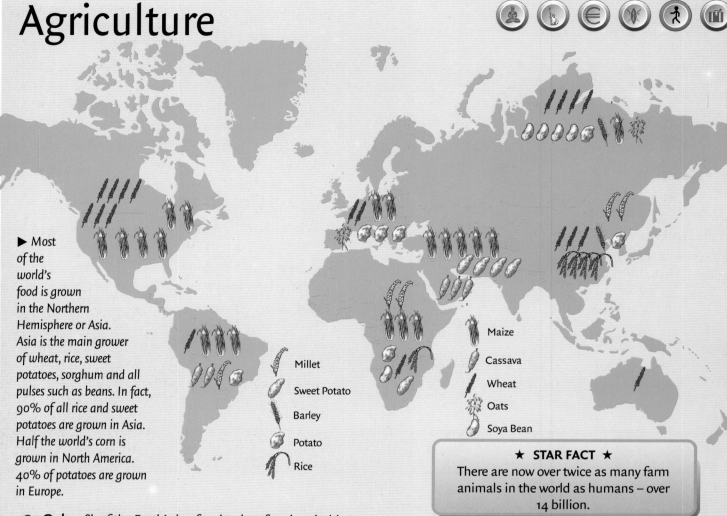

▶ Most of the world's food is grown in the Northern Hemisphere or Asia. Asia is the main grower of wheat, rice, sweet potatoes, sorghum and all pulses such as beans. In fact, 90% of all rice and sweet potatoes are grown in Asia. Half the world's corn is grown in North America. 40% of potatoes are grown in Europe.

Millet
Sweet Potato
Barley
Potato
Rice

Maize
Cassava
Wheat
Oats
Soya Bean

> ★ STAR FACT ★
> There are now over twice as many farm animals in the world as humans – over 14 billion.

- **Only 11%** of the Earth's ice-free land surface is suitable for growing crops – that is, about 13 billion hectares. The rest is either too wet or dry or cold, or has soil that is too shallow or poor in nutrients.

- **A much higher** proportion of Europe has fertile soil (36%) than any other continent. About 31% is cultivated.

- **In North America** 22% of the land is fertile but only 13% is cultivated, partly because much fertile land is lost under concrete. Surprisingly, 16% of Africa is potentially fertile, yet only 6% is cultivated.

- **Southern Asia** is so crowded that even though less than 20% of the land is fertile, over 24% is cultivated.

- **Dairy farms** produce milk, butter and cheese from cows in green pastures in fairly moist parts of the world.

- **Mixed farming** involves both crops and livestock as in the USA's Corn Belt, where farmers grow corn to feed pigs and cattle. Many European farms are mixed, too.

- **Mediterranean farming** is in areas with mild, moist winters and warm, dry summers – like California, Australia, South Africa and the Mediterranean. Here winter crops include wheat, barley and broccoli. Summer crops include peaches, citrus fruits, grapes and olives.

- **Shifting cultivation** involves growing crops like corn, rice, manioc, yams and millet in one place for a short while, then moving on before the soil loses goodness.

- **Shifting cultivation** is practised in the forests of Latin America, in Africa and parts of Southeast Asia.

◀ In places farming is now a highly mechanized industry, but in SE Asia many farmers work the land as they have for thousands of years.

# The West Indies

▶ Famous Jamaica rum is made from cane sugar, still the West Indies' major crop despite the rise of beet sugar.

- **Cuba:** Capital: Havana. Population: 10.9 million. Currency: Cuban peso. Language: Spanish.

- **Jamaica:** Capital: Kingston. Population: 2.5 million. Currency: Jamaican dollar. Language: English.

- **The four largest islands** in the West Indies are Cuba, Hispaniola, Jamaica and Puerto Rico. Hispaniola is split into two countries: Haiti and the Dominican Republic.

- **The islands** are mostly in a long curve stretching from Cuba to Trinidad. The Greater Antilles are the islands of the western end. The Lesser Antilles are the eastern end.

- **The original inhabitants** of the West Indies were Carib and Arawak peoples. Most died soon after the Spanish arrived in the 1500s from disease and abuse.

- **Today most West Indians** are descended from Africans brought here as slaves to work on the sugar plantations.

- **The slaves** were freed in the mid-1800s, but most people here are still poor and work for low wages.

- **In Haiti** only one person in 250 has a car; fewer than 1 in 10 has a phone.

- **Half** the people work the land. Many work on sugar, banana or coffee plantations, and also farm a plot to grow their own food.

- **Many tourists** come for the warm weather and clear blue seas.

# Vietnam and neighbours

- **Vietnam:** Capital: Hanoi. Population: 72.5 million. Currency: New dong. Language: Vietnamese.

- **Laos:** Capital: Vientiane. Population: 4.6 million. Currency: Kip. Language: Lao.

- **Cambodia:** Capital: Phnom Penh. Population: 10 million. Currency: Riel. Language: Khmer.

- **Indonesia:** Capital: Jakarta. Population: 194 million. Currency: Rupiah. Main language: Bahasa Indonesia.

◀ Warm and damp, Southeast Asia is a fertile region where Buddhist and Hindu kings once built giant temples in the forests, but many people today are desperately poor.

- **Laos, Vietnam and Cambodia** were once French colonies and the end of French rule in the 1950s led to years of suffering and war.

- **Both Laos and Vietnam** are one-party communist states, although their governments are elected by popular vote. In Cambodia, the king was restored to power in 1993.

- **Many people** in Laos and Vietnam are poor and live by growing rice. Laos is the world's poorest country.

- **In Indonesia,** an elected president has replaced dictator General Suharto but the military still have great power.

- **Spread over 13,677 islands,** Indonesia is one of the world's most densely populated countries. Jakarta is home to 7 million, and is heavily industrialized. In the country hillside terraces ensure every inch is used for rice.

- **Indonesian rainforest** is being rapidly destroyed by loggers. In 1997, the country was engulfed by smoke from fires started by loggers.

# Malaysia and Singapore

- **Malaysia:** Capital: Kuala Lumpur. Pop: 21 million. Curr: Malaysian dollar (ringgit). Language: Bahasa Malaysia.

- **Singapore:** Capital: Singapore. Population: 3.4 million. Currency: Singapore dollar. Languages: English, Mandarin, Malay and Tamil.

- **Malaysia** is split into sections: peninsular Malaysia and Sarawak and Sabah on the island of Borneo.

- **In the 1980s** Malaysia was a farming country relying on rubber for exports.

- **Malaysia** is still the world's top rubber producer.

- **Cheap, skilled labour** and oil have turned Malaysia into one of the world's most rapidly developing economies – as the new skyscrapers in Kuala Lumpur show.

- **A plan called 2020 Vision** aims to have Malaysia fully developed by the year 2020.

- **Singapore** may be the world's busiest port. Huge ships

▲ *Singapore is one of the busiest and most prosperous cities in Asia.*

tie up here every 3 minutes, day and night.

- **Singapore** is also one of Asia's most successful trading and manufacturing centres.

- **Singapore** has a state-of-the-art transport system, kept immaculately clean by strict laws governing litter.

# Peoples of Europe

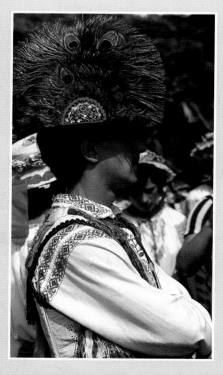

- **About 700 million** people live in Europe – about 12% of the world's population.

- **Europe** is one of the most densely populated continents averaging 67 people per square kilometre.

- **Most Europeans** are descended from tribes who migrated into Europe more than 1,500 years ago.

◄ *In East Europe, many people, like these Romanians, have their own traditional dress.*

- **Most British people** are descended from a mix of Celts, Angles, Saxons, Danes and others. Most French people are descended from Gauls and Franks. Most Eastern Europeans are Slavic (see peoples of Northern Asia).

- **North Europeans** such as Scandinavians often have fair skin and blonde hair. South Europeans such as Italians often have olive skin and dark hair.

- **Most European countries** have a mix of people from all parts of the world, including former European colonies in Africa and Asia.

- **Most Europeans** are Christians.

- **Most Europeans** speak an Indo-European language, such as English, French or Russian.

- **Languages** like French, Spanish and Italian are romance languages that come from Latin, language of the Romans.

- **Basque people** in Spain speak a language related to no other language. Hungarians, Finns and Estonians speak a Uralic-Altaic language like those of Turkey and Mongolia.

# Chile

- **Capital:** Santiago. Area: 756,945 sq km. Currency: Chilean peso. Language: Spanish.

- **Physical features:** Highest mountain: Ojos del Salado (6,908 m). Longest river: Bio-Bio (200 km).

- **Population:** 14.6 million. Population density: 19/sq km. Life expectancy: men 72.3 years; women 78.3 years.

- **Wealth:** GDP: $77 billion. GDP per head: $4,820.

- **Exports:** Copper, iron, fresh fruit, wood pulp.

- **Chile** is one of the world's most volcanically active countries, with 75 active volcanoes. Chile also has eight of the world's highest active volcanoes, including Guallatir (6,170 m) – the world's tallest.

- **Chile is a major** wine producer.

- **The copper mine** at Chuquicamata is the world's biggest man-made hole, 4 km long and 670 m deep. The El Teniente copper mine is the world's deepest.

- **Chile is the** world's largest copper producer.

- **The Mapuche Indians** live in the forest area around Temuco in southern Chile and those who preserve their traditional way of life live in round straw houses.

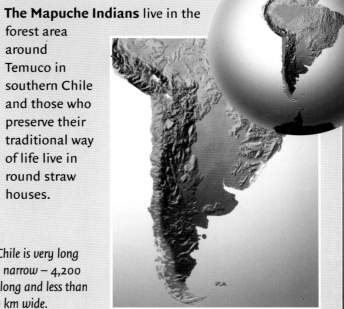

▶ Chile is very long and narrow – 4,200 km long and less than 180 km wide.

# Spain and Portugal

- **Spain:** Capital: Madrid. Area: 504,782 sq km. Currency: Peseta. Language: Spanish.

- **Physical features:** Highest mountain: Mulhacén (3,478 m). Longest river: Tagus (1,007 km).

- **Population:** 39.6 million. Population density: 78/sq km. Life expectancy: men 74.5 years; women 81.5 years.

- **Wealth:** GDP: $569.6 billion. GDP per head: $14,490.

- **Exports:** Cars, wine, machinery, fruit, olive oil, steel, textiles, chemicals.

- **Much of the centre of Spain** is too hot and dry for some crops, but perfect for olives, sunflowers and for grapes, oranges and other fruit. Spain is one of the world's leading fruit-growers.

- **Spain is one of the leading** carmakers in Europe, with huge plants in Valencia and Saragossa. It also makes a lot of iron and steel. Toledo in the south was once famous for its fine sword steel.

- **Portugal:** Capital: Lisbon. Population: 9.9 million. Currency: Escudo. Language: Portuguese.

- **Portugal** once had a large empire including large parts of Latin America and Africa. Yet it is fairly underdeveloped. Most people still live in the countryside, growing wheat, rice, almonds, olives and maize. Portugal is famous for its 'port', a drink made by adding brandy to wine.

◀ Spain and Portugal are isolated from the rest of Europe by the Pyrenees on their own peninsula, called Iberia. Europe's most westerly point, Cabo da Roca, is in Portugal.

★ STAR FACT ★
Every summer, 55 million sunseekers come to the beaches of Spain's Costa del Sol.

# Scandinavia

▲ *Norway's mountainous coast has been gouged into deep fjords by glaciers.*

- **Norway:** Capital: Oslo. Population: 4.4 million. Currency: Norwegian krone. Language: Norwegian.
- **Sweden:** Capital: Stockholm. Population: 8.9 million. Currency: Swedish krona. Language: Swedish.

- **Denmark:** Capital: Copenhagen. Population: 5.3 million. Currency: Danish krone. Language: Danish.
- **Finland:** Capital: Helsinki. Population: 5.1 million. Currency: Markka. Languages: Finnish and Swedish.
- **Scandinavia** has among the iciest, most northerly inhabited countries in the world. Yet they enjoy a high standard of living and welfare provision.
  - **Norway's fishing boats** land 2.4 million tonnes of fish a year – more than those of any other European country except Russia.
  - **Sweden is known** for its high-quality engineering, including its cars such as Volvos and aircraft-makers such as Saab.
  - **Finland and Sweden** are known for their glass and ceramic work.
- **Sweden's capital Stockholm** is built on four islands in an archipelago of 24,000 islands.
- **Danish farms** are famous for butter and bacon.

# Political systems

▶ *Bill Clinton was President of the USA from 1992-2000.*

- **Democracies** are countries with governments elected every few years by popular vote.
- **Most democracies** have a constitution, a written set of laws saying how a government must be run.
- **Democracies** like France are republics. This means the head of state is an elected president. In some republics like the USA, the president is in charge; in others, the president is a figurehead and the country is run by a chancellor or prime minister.

- **Monarchies** are countries which still have a monarch – a king or queen – like Britain. But their power is usually limited and the country is run by an elected government.
- **In autocracies** a single person or small group of people hold all the power, as in China and North Korea.
- **Most governments** are split into the legislature who make or amend laws, the executive who put them into effect and the judiciary who see they are applied fairly.
- **Most countries** are capitalist, which means most things – capital – are owned by individuals or small groups.
- **A few countries** like Cuba are communist, which means everything is owned by the community, or rather the state.
- **Socialists** believe the government should ensure everyone has equal rights, a fair share of money, and good health, education and housing.
- **Fascists** believe in rigid discipline and that they and their country are superior to others, like Hitler's Germany in the 1930s. There is no openly fascist country at present.

# The Pacific Islands

- **Scattered** around the Pacific are countless islands – maybe 20,000 or 30,000. Some are little more than rocks; some are thousands of square kilometres.

- **The Pacific Islands** altogether are sometimes known as Oceania, but they are in three main groups: Melanesia, Micronesia and Polynesia.

- **Melanesia** includes New Guinea, the Solomons, New Caledonia, Vanuatu and Fiji.

- **Melanesia** means 'black islands' and gets its name from the dark skin of many of the islanders here.

- **Micronesia** is 2,000 islands to the north of Melanesia, including Guam and the Marshall Islands.

- **Micronesia** means 'tiny islands'.

- **Polynesia** is a vast group of islands 8,000 km across. It includes Tahiti and Easter Island.

- **Polynesia** means 'many islands'.

- **Most of the islands** in the Pacific are either extinct volcanoes, or coral islands built around a volcanic peak. Atolls are coral rings left as the volcano sinks.

- **Most Pacific islanders** still live in small farming or fishing villages as they have for thousands of years, but western influences are changing the island way of life rapidly.

◄ *Like many Pacific islands, Fiji seems like a paradise.*

# Mexico

- **Capital:** Mexico City. Area: 1,972,545 sq km. Currency: Mexican peso. Language: Spanish.

- **Physical features:** Highest mountain: Citlaltépetl (5,700 m). Longest river: Rio Bravo (2,100 km).

- **Population:** 94.3 mill. Population density: 47/sq km. Life expectancy: men 69.5 years; women 75.5 years.

- **Wealth:** GDP: $348.6 billion. GDP per head: $3,700.

- **Exports:** Petroleum, vehicles, machinery, cotton, coffee, fish, fertilizers, minerals.

- **Mexico** is quite mountainous and only 12% of the land is suitable for farming, but the soil that develops on lava poured out by Mexico's many volcanoes is very fertile. Where there is enough rain, there are big plantations for tobacco, coffee, cane, cocoa, cotton and rubber.

- **Over half Mexico's** export earnings come from manufactured goods – notably cars.

- **Mexico has** a rapidly growing population. The birth rate is high and half the population is under 25.

- **Most of Mexico's people** are *mestizos* – descended from both American Indians and Europeans. But there are still 15 million American Indians.

- **Mexico City** is one of the world's biggest, busiest, dirtiest cities. The urban area has a population of over 16 million – and it is growing rapidly as more people move in from the country to find jobs.

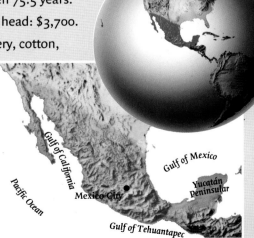

Gulf of California

Pacific Ocean

Mexico City

Gulf of Mexico

Yucatán Peninsular

Gulf of Tehuantapec

◄ *Mexico lies immediately south of the USA, between the Gulf of Mexico and the Pacific.*

# Mediterranean food

- **Mediterranean food** depends on ingredients grown in the warm Mediterranean climate. It tends to be lighter than north European food, including salads, flat bread and fish rather than sauces and stews.

- **Olive oil** is used for dressing salads and frying food.
- **There are five major styles** of Mediterranean food: Italian, Greek, Turkish, Spanish and North African.

◀ *Spaghetti Bolognese – spaghetti pasta with meat and tomato sauce – is the centrepiece of a typical Italian meal.*

- **Italian meals** often include pasta, which is made from durum wheat flour and served with a sauce.
- **Popular forms of pasta** include spaghetti ('little strings'), vermicelli ('little worms'), fusilli ('spindles') and tube-shaped macaroni.
- **In north Italy** ribbon pastas served with cream sauces are popular. In the south, macaroni served with tomato-based sauces are more popular.
- **Pizzas** are popular snacks, especially in the south.
- **Greek food** includes meats – especially lamb – and fish cooked in olive oil.
- **Greek salad** includes olives, cucumber, tomatoes, herbs and feta cheese (soft goat's cheese).
- **Spanish food** often includes seafood such as *calamares* (squid). *Paella* includes seafoods and chicken combined with rice and cooked in saffron. *Gazpacho* is a cold tomato soup. *Tapas* are small snacks, originating in northern Spain.

# Pakistan and Bangladesh

- **Pakistan:** Capital: Islamabad. Population: 144.1 million. Currency: Pakistan rupee. Language: Urdu.
- **Bangladesh:** Capital: Dhaka. Population: 122.7 million. Currency: Taka. Language: Bengali.
- **The Punjab** region is where many Pakistanis live. It gets its name – which means 'five waters' – from five tributaries of the River Indus: the Jhelum, Chenab, Ravi, Sutlej and Beas. These rivers water the Punjab's plains and make it fertile. All the same, large areas of the Punjab are dry and rely on one of the world's biggest irrigation networks.
- **Pakistan's major exports** include textiles, cement and machine tools.

▶ *Pakistan and Bangladesh were once one nation, East and West Pakistan, but East Pakistan broke away in 1971 to become Bangladesh.*

- **Buses, lorries and rickshaws** in Pakistan are decorated with colourful patterns, pictures of film stars and religious themes. Many people think that the better the vehicle looks, the more careful the driver will be.
- **Pakistan's capital** is the brand new city of Islamabad, built in the 1960s, but its biggest city and industrial centre is the port of Karachi.
- **While people in India** are mainly Hindu, in Pakistan and Bangladesh they are mainly Muslim.

- **Jute is a reed** that thrives in Bangladesh's warm, moist climate. It is used for making rope, sacking and carpet backing.
- **Over 70 big jute mills** make jute Bangladesh's most important export.
- **Most of Bangladesh** is low-lying and prone to flooding. Floods have devastated Bangladesh several times in the past 40 years.

# Switzerland and Austria

- **Switzerland:** Capital: Berne. Population: 7.3 million. Currency: Franc. Languages: German, French and Italian.
- **Austria:** Capital: Vienna. Population: 8.1 million. Currency: Schilling. Language: German.
- **Switzerland and Austria** are small but beautiful countries mostly in the Alps mountains.
- **Both Switzerland and Austria** make a great deal of money from tourists who come to walk and ski here.
- **Switzerland** has long been 'neutral', staying out of all the major wars. This is why organizations like the Red Cross and World Health Organization are based there.
- **Switzerland is** the world's richest country in terms of GDP per person ($43,060).
- **People from** all over the world put their money in Swiss banks because the country is stable politically and its banking laws guarantee secrecy.
- **Switzerland is famous** for making small, valuable things such as precision instruments and watches.

- **Vienna** was once the heart of the great Austrian Empire and the music capital of Europe.
- **Austrians** rely on mountain-river hydroelectricity for much of its power.

◄ *Austria earns more than a sixth of its income from tourists who come to enjoy the Alpine scenery.*

# New England

▲ *New England is famous for the stunning colours of its trees in 'fall' (autumn), when the leaves turn reds, golds and ambers.*

- **New England** is six states in northeast USA – Maine, Vermont, New Hampshire, Massachusetts, Rhode Island and Connecticut.
- **New England** was one of the first areas of North America settled by Europeans in the 1600s.

- **The USA's** oldest buildings are in New England.
- **New England** is famous for its attractive small towns with pretty 18th- and 19th-century white clapperboard houses and elegantly spired churches.
- **Vermont's** name means 'green mountain' and it has fewer urban inhabitants than any other state.
- **Basketball** was invented in Massachusetts in 1891.
- **Route 128** in Massachusetts is famed for its cutting-edge electronic technology factories.
- **Boston** is one of the USA's oldest, most cultured cities. It also has a large number of educational and research institutes. Harvard University is at Cambridge nearby. Yale is in Connecticut.
- **New Hampshire** is famous for its scenery.

> ★ **STAR FACT** ★
> Rhode Island is the smallest state in the USA, which is why it is often called 'Little Rhody'.

# INDEX

## ACKNOWLEDGEMENTS

**Artists:** The publishers thank the following sources for the use of their photographs:
Page 8 (T/L) Wolfgang Kaehler/CORBIS; Page 8 (B/L) Patrick Johns/CORBIS; Page 11 (B/L) Wolfgang Kaehler/CORBIS; Page 14 (B/C) Paul A. Souders/CORBIS; Page 16 (T/C) Guy Stubbs, Gallo Images/CORBIS; Page 21 (B/R) Panos Pictures; Page 26 (B/L) Catherine Karnow/CORBIS; Page 33 (T/R) Ted Atkinson, Eye Ubiquitous/CORBIS; Page 39 (B/L) John Batholomew/CORBIS; Page 40 (B/L) Panos Pictures; Page 41 (B/R) Guy Stubbs, Gallo Images/CORBIS; Page 44 (T/L) David Cumming, Eye Ubiquitous/CORBIS; Page 47 (B/C) Jeffrey L. Rotman/CORBIS; Page 49 (C/L) Daewoo Cars Ltd.; Page 50 (B/L) Owen Franken/CORBIS; Page 51 (T/R) London Aerial Photo Library/CORBIS; Page 53 (B/R) Fancoise de Mulder/CORBIS; Page 54 (T/L) Kelly-Mooney Photography/CORBIS; Page 56 (B/L) Charles & Josette Lenars/CORBIS.
All other photographs are from MKP Archive.